THE INSIDER RAIL GUI

Aberdeen to Elgin &

David Fasken and David Spave.

KESSOCK BOOKS

First published in Great Britain by Kessock Books 2017
Copyright © David Fasken and David Spaven 2017

The right of David Fasken and David Spaven to be considered as authors of this work
has been asserted by them in accordance with the Copyright, Designs and Patents Act 1988.

A CIP catalogue record for this book is available from the British Library

ISBN 978-0-9930296-9-1

Cover design by Audiografix
Text design and typesetting by Stanford DTP
Printed and bound in Great Britain by CPI Group (UK), Croydon, CR40 4YY

Contents

Acknowledgements

As well as our own knowledge of the railway, gathered over more than 50 years – and my research for *If Goalposts Could Talk....The Life & Times of Inverurie Locomotive Works Football Club* – this guide has benefited enormously from the detailed research and writing of a variety of authors. (*See Further Reading in Chapter Five.*)

The text is largely my responsibility, but David Spaven and I exchanged many insights on the road to final publication. We also travelled the line again together in Spring 2017 to bring our observations fully up to date, and then supplemented the rail experience with a car-based trip to capture on camera some of the finer detail of this wonderful working line.

The book has benefited from the considered craft of Alan Young's hand-drawn maps, which in turn are fittingly complemented by Merrill MacWilliam's evocative sketches of railway structures.

This has been very much a team effort.

David R. Fasken
Forgue,
Huntly,
Aberdeenshire
August 2017

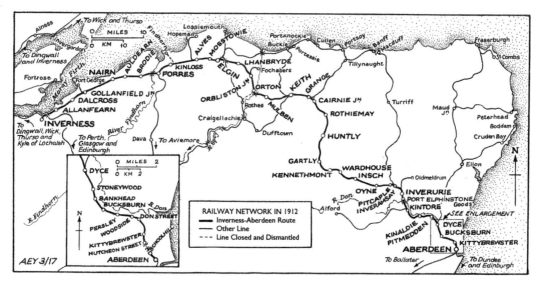

Alan Young's hand-drawn map shows the heyday of the Aberdeen-Inverness line and branches, just before World War One. The Great North of Scotland Railway (GNSR) network radiating out of Aberdeen has been characterised as 'all branch line', in contrast to the Highland Railway's as 'all main line': an over-simplification, but broadly reflecting the impact of the different physical and settlement geographies on the rail networks of each region. *Alan Young*

Introduction

The line from Aberdeen to Inverness is one of Scotland's lesser-known and unsung railways.

Unobtrusively tucked away on the north-east shoulder of the country, it links the Granite City with the Highland Capital and it is not, and has never had aspirations to be, one of the great scenic railway journeys of Scotland. That honour belongs to the West Highland Lines from Glasgow to Oban, Fort William and Mallaig, and the North Highland Lines from Inverness north to Wick and Thurso and west to Kyle of Lochalsh.

However, it is wrong to assume that this line suffers from any sense of inferiority. It serves a different purpose to the more glamorous lines. It is, and always has been, a relatively successful railway serving small and large communities along its path. Both passenger and freight traffic have been instrumental to its development and survival down the years.

This is a hard-working railway, regularly transporting people with busy professional and private lives, and yet it is also an interesting and intriguing line. This *Insider Guide* is written for the visitor and tourist, as well as for regular passengers.

We won't distract you with technicalities, but we will draw your attention to some of the history which underpins today's railway, and its distinctive architectural and operational quirks. We will also suggest how best to plan your journey and how to make the most of the view from your window.

The *Insider Rail Guides* are written by two authors steeped in Highland railways. Both have written a variety of books, notably David Spaven's *The Railway Atlas of Scotland* and *Highland Survivor: the story of* the *Far North Line;* and David Fasken's *Light Hearted Lines,* recounting tales of rail travel around Inverness in the 1960s and 1970s, and *If Goalposts Could Talk....The Life and Times of Inverurie Locomotive Works Football Club.*

CHAPTER ONE

A history of the line

Before the railway

The north-east of Scotland – the region encompassing the lands lying between the cities of Aberdeen and Inverness, and from the Moray Firth to the foothills of the Grampian mountains – is generally flat and fertile. It is, therefore, unsurprising that it has long been associated with agriculture.

A regular cattle trade had been established by the early 17th century, and fairs appeared at Turriff on the Deveron, Rayne in the Garioch, Kincardine on Deeside, and Deer in Buchan. Cattle, horses, sheep and coarse woollen cloth were sold at these markets.

The area's development was not dominated to the same extent by the traditional clan system which held sway over much of the area to the north and particularly to the west of Inverness. Also, the region was less badly affected by the 'withdrawal symptoms' resulting from the Jacobite defeat at the Battle of Culloden in 1746, as the government actively sought finally to bring the Highlands of Scotland under central state control.

The north-east had long been subject to cattle raiding from the west, and now the authorities turned their attention to its protection. Trade developed to the south, albeit slowly, via several routes, of which the main one was the high road over Cairn o' Mount between Banchory and Fettercairn. However, major agricultural development, including cattle breeding, was slow to progress during the 18th century. The counties of Aberdeenshire and Morayshire remained impoverished backwaters. The land was barren, and poor tenant farmers tilled a few narrow ridges of sparse arable land. Implements were primitive and methods backward due to the isolation of most rural communities. Often people and animals starved if the harvest failed. Communications were limited. From Huntly, it took heavy horse and cart six days to complete the 76-mile round trip to Aberdeen and back, usually to convey oats for sale in the city and to return with lime fertiliser.

Towards the end of the 18th century, however, Scotland's cities and towns were expanding, and growing demand for farm produce led to agricultural reform and increased efficiency. Much of the countryside was being transformed into enclosed, green, fertile fields, well protected by walls and trees. New crops such as turnip, potato, peas, and clover, were introduced. The Aberdeen-Inverurie canal opened in 1805, reducing the journey time from Huntly to Aberdeen to two days. By the 1820s higher crop yields and increasing prices were leading to great improvements in housing and standards of living. New roads were appearing across the region.

The railway arrives

As the 'railway mania' of the 1840s heralded numerous construction projects throughout Britain, promotion of railways also took hold in the north of Scotland. In 1845 the Highland engineer Joseph Mitchell proposed a route south from Inverness to Perth. He was, however, ahead of his time, as Parliament expressed incredulity at the projected gradients over the Grampian Mountains and firmly rebuffed his proposal. The

An early-20th century photograph of Inverurie Station, built in 1902, looking towards Aberdeen. The island platform features distinctive awnings over the platform buildings, and the middle rail track of the main line allows through trains to bypass those on the platform tracks. The bay platform for the Oldmeldrum branch line train (hauled by an engine known affectionately as 'Meldrum Meg') is on the left. *Local Studies Department of Aberdeenshire Library in Oldmeldrum*

following year Mitchell turned his attention to an alternative route south via Aberdeen. That route would be longer, but easier. His first target was Nairn, 16 miles east of Inverness.

In that same year, 1846, Parliament approved the Great North of Scotland Railway Bill, and Inverness found itself the target of interests in the Granite City. Leading Aberdeen politicians and businessmen were determined that any railway development around and from that city would be promoted by local, and not by outside, interest.

The race was now on. The Great North of Scotland Railway Company in Aberdeen and (what was to become) the Highland Railway Company in Inverness eyed each other's territory enviously. The goal for the Great North was the first route to the Highlands from the south, and for the Highland the reverse. Both recognised the not inconsiderable geographical barrier of the Grampian Mountains between Perth and Inverness.

In 1850 Aberdeen was reached by the Aberdeen Railway from the south (Dundee). The separate Great North of Scotland Railway north to Huntly, initially single-track, was completed in 1854. There were passing loops at Kintore, Inverurie and Insch. Due to financial constraints on capital, the first Great North terminus was built north of the city centre at Kittybrewster, but it proved less than satisfactory.

Despite a main road connection (George Street), it was a mile from the city centre and had no link with the harbour or with the Aberdeen Railway at Guild Street. Therefore, in 1856 a one and three-quarter-mile branch to a new terminus at Waterloo on the harbour was opened to passengers. The line northwards was subsequently doubled: to Dyce in 1861, Kintore in 1880, Inveramsay in 1882, Insch in 1888, Huntly in 1896, and Keith in 1898.

The Inverness and Nairn Railway opened in 1855 and a third company, the Inverness and Aberdeen Junction Railway, was formed to push on eastwards to challenge the Great North. And so it came to pass

The Aberdeen suburban station of Kittybrewster once featured a distinctive example of GNSR station architecture, captured in this sketch of a 1952 scene. Flanking the station (closed in 1968) were a large locomotive depot and goods marshalling yards, all of which have gone today, but Kittybrewster remains the junction for the freight branch line to Waterloo Quay. *Merrill MacWilliam (from a photo by HC Casserley)*

An undated pre-1948 photograph of the exterior frontage of the GNSR's Elgin East Station, which served trains to Lossiemouth and to Aberdeen via Buckie ('Coast Line') and via Craigellachie ('Glen Route'). The 'baronial' architecture is impressive, and the railway posters, milk churns and luggage trolleys – and the absence of motor vehicles – all illustrate a bygone age. However, although all passenger train services were withdrawn in 1968, the B-Listed building remains well-preserved today as a business centre. *Great North of Scotland Railway Association*

The GNSR station at Elgin East had one through platform (on the left, from the Highland Railway station at Elgin West), and three bay platforms (on the right). On 25 April 1952, B1 No. 61345 prepares to depart with the 9.12 train to Aberdeen via Craigellachie. *HC Casserley*

in 1858 that they met head-on at Keith, more or less the midway point, as the final link from Nairn was completed in only two years. A railway of 108½ miles was in place between the Granite City and the Highland Capital, but the Great North had failed to achieve its objective of completing the entire line to Inverness. The two companies subsequently shared a troubled relationship, especially at Keith. It would be 90 years before the line was 'unified' under the Scottish Region of British Railways as a result of Nation-alisation in 1948.

'Great North' and 'Highland' rivalry

Joseph Mitchell faced a dilemma. The Highland Railway Company experienced difficulty in securing through-running of trains from Inverness to the south via Keith and Aberdeen due to the uncooperative Great North. Furthermore, until 1867, the line into Aberdeen terminated at Waterloo, half a mile distant from Guild Street, where trains from and to the south arrived and departed. Although a special horse-drawn omnibus connected the two stations, it proved notoriously unreliable, and passengers were often left to find their own way. The inconvenient transfer and poor connections forced Mitchell to revisit his direct line south.

A new company, the Inverness and Perth Junction Railway, was established and the Highland Main Line from Perth to Inverness opened in 1863. That provided a fresh impetus to establish an easier interchange between the railways north and south of Aberdeen. In November 1867 a new line through the Denburn Valley, involving two tunnels, linked Kittybrewster directly with a new station adjacent to Guild Street, and immediately effected a great improvement. The station became known to generations of Aberdonians as the

This undated 1960s view of the north end of Aberdeen (Joint) illustrates the once-extensive track layout, with its four through and four bay platforms and goods sidings to the left. Following the withdrawal of passenger services to Fraserburgh and Peterhead (in 1965) and local passenger services on the main line to Elgin (in 1968), redevelopment work in the early 1970s removed two through platforms and all the goods sidings and bay platforms. *Great North of Scotland Railway Association*

'Joint Station', as it was shared, initially with the Scottish North Eastern Railway, and subsequently by three of Scotland's five main railway companies: the Great North, Caledonian and North British.

The revised arrangements in Aberdeen, however, counted for little. The new and shorter Highland Main Line route from Inverness to Perth attracted most of the southbound traffic, including the valuable mail contract. Moreover, the Great North initially had a poor reputation for service, and its shareholding in the Inverness and Edinburgh Steam Packet Company at Waterloo led to agricultural produce being despatched south by sea, with the company even refusing to quote through rates by rail.

However, the industries of Aberdeen benefited immediately from the railway. In addition to the established textile industry, there developed paper making and engineering (including the production of machinery for local farms, granite quarries and paper mills). It was envisaged that the city would become a consignment centre for fish to be delivered by rail for onward shipment to southern markets by sea. In fact, the opposite happened as fish was transferred from boat to rail. This business was limited initially, as much of the catch was cured locally, but, as steam trawlers led to Aberdeen developing as a major fishing port from the 1890s, the conveyance of fish increased significantly. Fish were sold in Billingsgate within 24 hours of being landed in Aberdeen. The local fleet grew from 40 to 178 vessels in the 10 years from 1894.

The ill-feeling and lack of co-operation at Keith between the Great North and the Highland Railway Company (formed in 1865 through a merger of the Inverness and Aberdeen Junction and the Inverness and Perth Junction Railway Companies) lasted well into the 20th century, although the relationship did improve after 1900. The Great North was still determined, however, to push on further westwards, and subsequently did so by acquiring two alternative lines to Elgin: via Dufftown, Craigellachie and Rothes in 1863 (the 'Glen Route'); and via Cullen and Buckie in 1886 (the 'Coast Line').

The 'Scottish Railtour' pauses in Aberdeen on 14 June 1960, with GNSR Class F 4-4-0 No. 49 *Gordon Highlander* in charge. Built by the North British Locomotive Company in Glasgow in 1920, she was designed to haul 'mixed traffic' (ie both passenger and goods trains) and was based in Keith for much of her working life. *Gordon Highlander* was known locally by her nickname 'The Sodger' (soldier), and, although retired by British Railways in 1957, she continued to haul excursion trains until 1966. The locomotive is now owned by the Glasgow Museum of Transport, and is currently on static display with the Scottish Railway Preservation Society at Bo'ness. *HC Casserley*

A modern diesel-multiple-unit (DMU) is about to depart from Kintore Station, between Dyce and Inverurie. This is thought to be a Branch Line Society special which toured the Alford, Oldmeldrum and Turriff branches on 5 June 1965. Kintore was the junction for the 16-mile line to Alford which closed to passengers in 1950 and to freight in 1966. Kintore itself closed in 1964, but following major housing development over the past 40 years, it is proposed to re-open the station. *Great North of Scotland Railway Association*

A 1967 scene which is unrecognisable today. Forres was a triangular station, being the junction of the Highland Railway's main line south to Perth via Dava Moor and Grantown-on-Spey, and its 'branch' to Keith. This photograph taken from the south clearly shows the lines (and platforms) connecting west to Inverness and east to Aberdeen. The station building towards the western point of the triangle, built in 1955, is now closed, following completion of the track realignment and station relocation project in late 2017. *David Spaven*

The railway network develops

However, the Great North progressed no further than Elgin and subsequently concentrated on a series of branch lines serving both the coastal communities of Lossiemouth (1852), Banff (1859), Peterhead (1862), Fraserburgh (1865), Macduff (1872), Boddam (1896), and St Combs (1903), as well as the agricultural centres of Oldmeldrum (1856), Alford (1859), and Ballater (1866). Most of these lines were promoted, and indeed built, by small local companies, but they had neither the finance nor expertise to operate them and were, within a relatively short time, absorbed by the Great North. There was a major consolidation as early as 1866.

The conveyance of fish, agricultural produce, and tourists complemented the day-to-day passenger business. The railway served the dispersed agricultural centres and small market towns, and was instrumental in the north-east of Scotland developing as a region renowned for fattening cattle. Trains brought in store cattle and fertiliser and conveyed fat cattle to market. Auction marts and agricultural supply companies appeared in railway towns such as Keith, Mulben and Dufftown. In 1866 the Speyside Line connected the Great North at Craigellachie to the original Highland Main Line at Boat of Garten. This line provided another route to the south and served many whisky distilleries. Timber was another source of freight business.

The Highland then turned its attention north (to Wick and Thurso) and west (to Kyle of Lochalsh). It did, however, construct four short branch lines from the main Inverness-Keith line to Findhorn (1860), Burghead (1862)/Hopeman (1892), Fochabers (1893) and Fort George (1899). Attracted by the thriving fishing industry in the Buckie area, it built an alternative link between Keith and Portessie in 1884. It was a

The scale of railway operations in the Highland Capital is well demonstrated in this winter 1967–68 shot, with a Class 26 slowing its train for arrival at Inverness Station. The vacant land on the left was the site of the steam roundhouse until 1960–61 and was subsequently developed as an extension to the cattle market and, more recently, as a supermarket. *David Spaven*

difficult route over the Enzie Braes, with a summit of 670 feet. The track was lifted as early as 1915 to help the war effort and, although subsequently re-laid, was never officially re-opened. The track was removed a second time in 1937 apart from a stump from Keith to connect with the nearby Aultmore Distillery. This short section closed in 1966, but the distillery continues in operation today. The Highland's aspirations to reach Aberdeen died at Keith, and that town became a bustling railway centre hosting the two railway companies and serving thriving whisky, textile, and agricultural industries.

The Aberdeen to Inverness line, therefore, was the proverbial 'line of two halves'. The fractious relationship between the Great North and the Highland companies rumbled on throughout the 19th century, manifesting itself particularly at the meeting points of Keith, Elgin and Boat of Garten. The Great North desperately wanted direct access into Inverness, but the Highland was equally determined to prevent that, and refused to consider the section from Forres to Keith as part of a main line. They viewed that as a branch from their main line south from Inverness to Perth via Forres and Dava Moor.

Disputes often led to arbitration and even litigation. Agreement to allow the transfer of through coaches resulted in further argument, with the Great North, for example, claiming their coaches were being used by 'locals' on the Highland section. The real loser was the fare-paying passenger, who was subjected to appalling connections and poor service from both companies. The feud did start to abate after further discussion and agreement in 1897, but a detailed proposal for a full merger of both companies in 1905 foundered on the distrust in Inverness of the Great North's true intentions, which were to transfer management and engineering to Aberdeen and Inverurie.

A southbound train prepares to depart from Platform 4 at Inverness in September 1975, seen from the concourse under the train shed (dating back to Highland Railway days), which still survives. Of the station's seven platforms, numbers 1 to 4 serve trains to the south and east. *Frank Spaven*

The wood-panelled booking hall in Aberdeen Station, with trademark GNSR barriers, is captured here on 19 May 1973. It was soon replaced by a characterless modern equivalent. *HC Casserley*

Traditional semaphore signal gantries span multiple tracks as the Angus Railway Group's 'Buchan Belle' DMU enters the south end of Aberdeen Station on 1 June 1974. The special train, which originated in Perth, would continue on the main line north to Dyce, then diverge on to the freight-only branch to Fraserburgh, which closed five years later. The signal box on the left – Aberdeen South, opened in 1947 – was one of six in the Aberdeen area which were replaced by a single power signalling centre in 1981. *Bill Roberton*

Grouping, nationalisation and Beeching

In 1923 all Britain's railways were consolidated into four large companies. This was known as the 'Grouping', but even after that the two halves of the Aberdeen-Inverness line were in different camps. One interesting and unique anomaly resulted. The Great North lines fell into the London & North Eastern Railway (LNER), but the entire area was separated completely from the rest of the LNER's system by 38 miles of London Midland Scottish Railway (LMSR) track south from Aberdeen to Kinnaber Junction, north of Montrose, over which they did, however, have 'running powers'. The Grouping resulted in further attempts to establish through coaches from the south, initially by the introduction of a sleeping car service from London King's Cross to Lossiemouth. This was the longest through working on Britain's network and it continued until 1939.

Nationalisation in 1948 finally brought the entire line (and indeed both areas) under the sole management of British Railways. From 1949 to 1962 weekly through coaches ran from Glasgow Buchanan Street to Elgin and Keith, and there was a short-lived service of through coaches from Edinburgh and London to Elgin. Such initiatives reflected the importance of tourist traffic to the Great North and its successors. The company developed train excursions such as the 'Speyside' running to Boat of Garten via Keith and Dufftown; and to Elgin via the coast.

But Dr. Richard Beeching lay in wait. He was the Chairman of the new British Railways Board from 1961 to 1965. The internal combustion engine had gradually been stealing market share from the railways all over the country, and increasing competition from buses and lorries, followed by an upsurge in private car ownership in the 1950s and 1960s, led to people abandoning the railways in droves. Early indications of the danger from road competition was apparent in the 1950s when an Aberdeen *Evening Express* journalist commented that, on the line between Keith and Elgin, the intermediate stations had seen better days

Welsh's Bridge signal box (one of five in Inverness) controlled an impressive gantry of semaphore signals, seen here from a train arriving from Aberdeen on 6 September 1986. A resignalling scheme in 1988 saw all five manual boxes replaced by an electronic control centre and colour-light signals. *Merrill MacWilliam (from a photo by Bill Roberton)*

and that traffic was sparse. He wrote: 'There was something rather pathetic in the way the gold braided Stationmasters walked the lengths of their platforms, shouting station names.'

The savage 'Beeching cuts' of the mid to late 1960s saw the Great North's mileage in north-east Scotland reduce from 336 to 130. All the Great North and Highland branches, without exception, closed to passengers and, from 1968, only the original main line between the two cities remained. Services were cut and passenger numbers diminished. Diesel multiple units had replaced steam on the Aberdeen – Inverness line in 1960, a great improvement at the time, but all double track was singled in 1971, apart from a short section between Insch and Kennethmont.

The journey time from Aberdeen to Inverness settled down to two and a half hours. Diesel locomotive-hauled trains took over in 1980 until the introduction of today's Sprinter units in 1990. Freight continued at much reduced levels as road competition hit hard. Maltings at Burghead and Roseisle kept the Alves to Burghead branch open until the early 1990s, while whisky-related goods, mainly barley, had been transported on the surviving Keith to Dufftown line until the early 1980s. Timber was moved on the main line until the early 2000s, but since then freight movements have been sporadic. However, following the closure of Guild Street freight depot in Aberdeen (adjacent to the passenger station) to make way for the Union Square shopping mall, a new freight terminal was opened in 2009 at Raith's Farm to the north of Dyce station. It has been handling oil pipes in recent years.

A modern railway evolves

The burgeoning North Sea Oil industry led to a boom in industrial and housing development along the route. That, combined with associated road congestion along the A96 corridor and rising fuel prices, has

The B-Listed four-roomed station building on the Aberdeen platform at Insch was saved from demolition and fully renovated in the mid-1990s. It is a rare example of traditional rural railway architecture, and since 1997 has housed the Insch Connection Museum. The centre of the building still acts as the station waiting room. *David Fasken*

Huntly signal box, seen from the south from a Class 47-hauled Aberdeen-Inverness service on 6 September 1986.
Bill Roberton

The Royal Scotsman luxury land-cruise train has long been a summer visitor to the Aberdeen-Inverness line, often stabling overnight at the former Dufftown branch platform. It is seen here on 30 September 2009, with the distinctive (for Britain) open verandah at the rear of the train's observation car. *Ewan Crawford*

led to a line reborn. Dyce station, closed in 1968, re-opened in 1984. Elgin, Keith and Huntly stations have been rebuilt, and Inverurie improved. A more regular commuter service in and out of Aberdeen has evolved in recent years by running some Edinburgh services through Aberdeen on to, first, Dyce and then Inverurie. An early morning commuter train from Huntly to Aberdeen was introduced in 2016.

Today, the line is operating at full capacity, serving regular commuters, shoppers, and visitors. The current journey time between the two cities is only slightly faster than when diesels were introduced in 1960, albeit still competitive with road transport. In part, this reflects the capacity issue of the single line, with some trains being scheduled to wait for several minutes in the loops to allow trains to cross each other. A current concern is that the Scottish Government's planned £3bn investment to dual the parallel A96 road will reduce the competitive position of the railway for end-to-end journeys.

There are, however, exciting proposals and plans for the line's future. Long-term objectives (by 2030) are to cut the end-to-end journey time from the current two hours and twenty-five minutes to just two hours and with an hourly service, and to open new stations at Kintore and Dalcross.

The first phase has installed modern signalling between Elgin and Nairn, extended the platforms at the former station, and relocated and rebuilt Forres station. Later phases will see track re-doubling between Aberdeen and Inverurie and the provision of enhanced commuter services to Aberdeen and Inverness. By 2018–19, the line will also see the deployment of refurbished Inter-City 125 trains on most services, offering higher standards of comfort and on-train facilities, and restoring the line's status as a key cross-Scotland inter-urban railway.

To the west side of Keith station (formerly Keith Junction) the railway runs between the whisky bonds of Chivas Regal. This view looking east towards Keith on 5 April 2017 shows the telegraph poles which adorn much of the Aberdeen-Inverness route, the last railway line in Britain to use this form of communication between signal boxes. *David Fasken*

Now a private residence, Gartly station – closed in 1968 – lies in Strathbogie between Kennethmont and Huntly. This view on 14 April 2017 shows the old Elgin-bound platform and the space formerly occupied by the double track which extended from Aberdeen to Keith until 1971. *David Fasken*

CHAPTER TWO

Preparing for your journey

The passenger train services between Aberdeen and Inverness are part of the ScotRail franchise, created by the controversial privatisation of Britain's railway in the mid-1990s. The current privatised ScotRail franchise – paid for by the Scottish Government to the tune of £7 billion over ten years – is operated by Abellio, ironically a subsidiary of the state-owned Dutch Railways.

The ScotRail website – www.scotrail.co.uk – contains much of the information you will need about train times, station facilities, and tickets. The printed 'Inverness – Aberdeen' pocket timetable is a useful companion to your journey, and is also reproduced on the ScotRail website.

When to travel

Bear in mind that this is a popular line. The early morning and evening trains are very busy with commuters and shoppers, and the weekday 17.26 departure from Aberdeen is a particular service to avoid. Trains tend to be less busy in the middle of the day and at weekends, but the best tactic, if possible, is to pre-book your seat.

There are 11 return services per day Monday to Saturday inclusive and therefore, if you are based in either Aberdeen or Inverness and with a total journey time within two and a half hours, it is very easy to make a return day trip to/from both cities or to/from any of the intermediate stops. All trains connecting the two cities call at all the intermediate stations. There is a Sunday service of five trains each way.

Given the vagaries of Scotland's weather it is difficult to recommend a particular time of year to travel. All seasons bring their own attraction, but April to September sees the longer hours of daylight and the greater chance of the sun making an appearance.

Buying your ticket/ticket types/seat reservations/assisted travel/bikes on trains

Some trains have both First and Standard Class accommodation, but others offer only Standard Class. Check the timetable when you are buying your ticket. Tickets can be bought on the day from ScotRail ticket offices at Aberdeen, Inverurie, Huntly, Keith, Elgin, Forres, Nairn and Inverness or, in the case of Dyce and Insch (which are unstaffed), from the guard on the train. Alternatively, you can buy tickets from the machines at all the intermediate stations. Note that the ticket offices may only be open for part of the day. Outwith opening hours, tickets can be bought from machine or train guard.

Note that all tickets for trains departing all stations on the Aberdeen–Inverness line before 09.30 Monday–Friday incur a premium 'peak' rate. It is, therefore, cheaper to plan your departure after 09.30 on these days to take advantage of 'off-peak' fares. The 17.14 from Inverness and the 17.26 from Aberdeen Monday to Friday departures also incur a 'peak' rate.

There is a relatively simple choice of ticket types for journeys wholly on the Aberdeen – Inverness line, including:

This April 2017 sketch shows Inverurie station, still in full use today. The coffee shop at the far end was the private waiting room, with penny-in-the-slot toilet, for the Earl of Kintore. One day, Stationmaster James Gregor rushed to the aid of an uncomfortable Earl who was short of change. In gratitude, the Earl presented him with a silver dish inscribed: 'A Friend In Need Is A Friend Indeed'. *Merrill MacWilliam (from a photo by David Fasken)*

- **Anytime Day Return:** a flexible ticket with no time restrictions on when you can travel, which can be booked in advance or purchased on the day of travel – but you must travel out and back on the stated day. You may start, break and resume, or end your journey at any intermediate station along the route. If you decide not to use your ticket to make all or part of your intended journey, then you can apply for a refund, subject to a £10 administration fee.
- **Anytime Return:** a fully flexible ticket, with the same conditions as the Anytime Day Return, except that the outward portions of Anytime Returns are valid for five days including the date on the ticket, and you can return anytime within a month.
- **Advance Purchase Single:** available on specified trains only, with no refunds.
- **Anytime Day Single:** a fully flexible ticket with no time restrictions on when you can travel, which can be booked in advance or purchased on the day of travel – but you must travel out on the stated day. Refunds available, subject to a £10 administration fee. This ticket type is only marginally cheaper than the Anytime Day Return.

All such tickets also benefit from the one-third Railcard reduction, e.g. for Senior Citizens, Families, or Young Persons. A fee is payable for such annual railcards, but it is worth checking at staffed stations for details of eligibility, cost, and benefits.

Two 'Rover Tickets' are available, both including the Aberdeen – Inverness line as well as other rail routes, plus some bus and ferry services:

The attractive scenery of the central section of the Aberdeen-Inverness line is captured in this photo taken on 19 April 2017 from the stone-built overbridge carrying the main driveway of the Wardhouse Estate, formerly the home of the Gordon family. The 13.38 train from Aberdeen rushes towards Kennethmont on the line's surviving six-mile double-track section, with the distinctive shape of Tap o' Noth in the distance. *David Fasken*

- **Highland Rover:** covering Aberdeen – Inverness, plus North Highland (Inverness to Kyle of Lochalsh and Wick/Thurso), and West Highland (Glasgow Queen Street to Oban, Fort William and Mallaig) lines. Offers four days unlimited travel over eight consecutive days.
- **Spirit of Scotland Travelpass:** covering the entire ScotRail network. Offers four days of unlimited travel over eight consecutive days, or eight out of 15 days.

Both tickets can be purchased from a ticket office at any staffed station, by phone on 0344 811 0141, or by completing an online form.

For complete peace of mind in advance – particularly if you are travelling at busy times – seat reservations can be obtained free of charge when you buy your travel ticket (but note that reservations cannot be made if you are purchasing a ticket for immediate travel).

If you require 'assisted travel', ScotRail can arrange assistance if, at least four hours in advance, you phone 0800 912 2901 (or text phone 18001 0800 912 2901 if you are hard of hearing).

Free bicycle reservations are available in advance, by booking online when you buy your rail ticket/calling telesales on 0344 811 0141/ visiting one of ScotRail's staffed stations.

Check that the travel/ticket conditions summarised above are applicable before you make a booking.

What should you take with you on the train?

If you intend to walk and/or explore any distance from stations on the line, then good footwear and wet weather protection are sensible precautions. Most, but not all, trains have buffet trolleys, so you may wish to

The B-listed Boat o' Brig over the River Spey between Keith and Elgin is seen from its south end on 5 April 2017. This steel-lattice girder viaduct was built by the Highland Railway Company in 1906 to replace Joseph Mitchell's original plate-girder construction of 1858. *David Spaven*

take your own food and drink. Binoculars and, more obviously, a camera are useful companions. Up to two dogs, including guide dogs, are allowed on trains free of charge, but they must be kept on a lead.

ScotRail's 'Inverness – Aberdeen' pocket timetable will allow you to keep track (no pun intended) of the train's timekeeping, and even to anticipate where and when trains will cross. Topographical maps, such as the Ordnance Survey (OS) 'Landranger' series (Sheets 26, 27, 28, 29, 37, and 38) – or the single 'Northern Scotland, Orkney & Shetland' sheet of the OS 'Travel Map' series - will help you to appreciate the view from the window.

And, of course, you are already in possession of the essential guide to the trip. So read on for our insights into making the most of your train and the journey to the Capital of the Highlands, and beyond....

Just upstream from the railway structure spanning the River Spey lies the Boat o' Brig carrying the B9103 road over the river. Not a train in sight, but this shot of a 44-tonne whisky lorry illustrates the wider benefits of proposals to switch Speyside freight traffic from truck to train. *David Spaven*

On 24 March 2017, Insch station awaits the 10.57 train from Inverness and the 12.00 from Aberdeen which will cross on this double-track section. The station is little changed since construction in 1880, and has largely been spared the proliferation of CCTV camera poles which intrude on many stations today. The hilltop castle of Dunnideer provides a distinctive backcloth to the north. *David Fasken*

CHAPTER THREE

Making the most of your journey

If you are joining the train at Aberdeen or Inverness, you will need to insert your ticket in the electronic ticket barriers which separate the station concourse from the platforms. The platform number is clearly indicated on the large departure/arrival board in the concourse. All other stations on the line are free from electronic control, and you can access the train without impediment.

The trains

The standard ScotRail trains serving the Aberdeen - Inverness line are the older Class 158 diesel unit in combinations of two or four coach formation, and the more modern Class 170 diesel unit in combinations of three or six coach formation. Both classes have engines slung under the floor, and occasionally a longer train is assembled from the two classes. The train class is clearly indicated by numbers on the front of the train.

Each coach has two sets of external doors: one at each end of the Class 158, while the doors of the Class 170 are one-third and two-thirds along the length of each coach. These are twin 'plug doors' which move out and along the side of the train. They cannot be opened until the train has come to a complete stop and the guard has centrally unlocked them – indicated by the push-button door switches lighting up. From the outside, the activating button is to the right of the doors on the Class 158, while on the Class 170 it is more conveniently located on the door itself. You should, for safety, always 'mind the gap'.

For passengers with a disability, with advance notice ScotRail will provide a ramp and appropriate assistance to enable unhindered access by wheelchair to the train. Arrive in plenty of time before the train departure. Train staff will guide you to the dedicated allocated wheelchair space, located on both classes of train towards the end of one of the coaches, although in slightly differing positions.

Within the Class 158 train there are further internal dividing doors. These are activated by a button to the right. The passenger accommodation comprises an open saloon with seats on either side of an open aisle. In both Class 158 and Class 170 trains, seats are generally grouped in 'bays' of four seats around a table (two facing towards and two with back to direction of travel), with the bay usually well matched to the window for optimum viewing. Other seats are 'airline' style, with two on each side of the central aisle either facing or with back to the direction of travel. The view from the train is generally not so good from 'airline' seats, due to the high seat backs.

For the discerning passenger, you can avoid being seated directly above the underfloor engines (towards the centre of the coach), but this will be at the price of a slightly rougher ride above the wheels (towards the ends of the coaches). In practice, the levels of noise and vibration anywhere in the Class 158s and 170s are not particularly noticeable, as these trains are sealed, air-conditioned units.

Within one of the coaches, usually towards one end, you will find a large multi-purpose space for wheelchair users, large items of luggage and bicycles. For most day trip purposes, there is adequate room for smaller luggage items in the overhead racks directly above the seats, and in the floor space between adjacent sets of four-seat bays. Don't leave luggage in the aisle or blocking doorways, as this will impede other passengers, staff and the buffet trolley, and could constitute a significant safety hazard.

Toilets are clearly indicated and are located at the end of the coach. There are two types. One is a fully accessible facility (allowing wheelchair access) with electronic door opened, closed and locked by push-buttons, while the other is smaller, with manual sliding lock.

On the journey

Before and during your journey, you will typically hear a range of public address announcements. Some are pre-recorded to advise general information about the train and the stops it will make, while others are made by the guard for line-specific purposes, such as prolonged waits (some of which are scheduled) to allow trains to cross. But, be warned. The quality of public address announcements remains inconsistent and patchy. The electronic signs in both Class 158 and Class 170 coaches indicates progress along the line and advance warning of the next station stop, but these suffer from occasional malfunction. Often it's best to revert to the convenient method of looking through your window.

The railways, of course, have their own sets of rules, regulations and operational procedures and these can be reflected in obscure jargon, even emanating from public announcements. Here is a selection of translations of some potentially confusing railway expressions:

- 'We are waiting for the road': derived from the original British description of 'railroad' (as still used today in the USA and Canada), this is a reference to waiting for clearance from signal control to enter the single-track section ahead, very often because a train travelling in the opposite direction is due in the crossing loop beside which your train is standing.

- 'We are waiting for the Up Train': on Britain's railways 'Up' describes trains heading towards London (or Edinburgh), while 'Down' describes trains travelling away from London (or Edinburgh). On the Aberdeen – Inverness line, 'Up' trains are eastbound, and 'Down' trains are westbound.
- 'Crossing loop': these are the short sections of double track, usually within stations, to allow trains to pass. On the Aberdeen - Inverness line, the loop at Keith is outside the station (to the east). There is currently only one section of double-track on the line: the six miles between Insch and Kennethmont, this being a residual section of the original line which was double-track all the way from Aberdeen to Keith.

Most on-train railway staff are happy to help customers with any queries or requests for information. While you are unlikely to see or hear the train driver, who is concentrating on his duties in the front cab, the guard will pass through the passenger accommodation to check tickets and provide travel information. If your train is running late and you have a rail connection at your destination, the guard may be able to provide you with updated information of what to do on arrival. Buffet trolleys are available on some, but not all, trains, and provide snacks and drinks to passengers at their seats. Check the availability of the catering service on your train before departure; and be aware that, on some of the longer trains, the catering trolley may only be available in part of the train. Note that the consumption of alcohol after 21.00 and before 10.00 is prohibited by law on all ScotRail trains.

While the 158s and 170s are sealed, air-conditioned units, you will be conscious of some engine noise, especially when pulling away from stations and on climbing gradients. However, the Aberdeen – Inverness line is relatively level for long stretches and, compared to the routes further north and west, steep climbs are relatively limited. Another sound you may notice occasionally, especially on either side of Huntly, is the

As seen on 5 April 2017, Nairn station has changed little since 1855, with its B-listed stone and wood buildings, metal footbridge and two signal boxes encapsulating the Victorian era. Until 1965 its long platforms also hosted through trains from Inverness to Edinburgh and Glasgow (and London on Sundays) via Forres and the original Highland Main Line over Dava Moor. *David Spaven*

distinctive 'clickety click' of the train's wheels on joints between the rails. Once familiar across Britain, this reassuring rhythm has largely disappeared from inter-city routes where short (60 feet length) rails have been replaced by long stretches of continuously welded track.

With regard to safety on your journey, rail is by far the safest overland form of transport. At the time of writing, no passenger had been killed in a main line train accident anywhere on Britain's railways since 2007. Single-track rail operation in the North of Scotland is a long-established and well-developed practice, whose safety has been continuously refined and enhanced, in part through learning the lessons of train accidents in the Victorian era. If safety is your main concern, especially over the congested and dangerous A96, then the train is far and away the best method of travel from Aberdeen to Inverness. In the unlikely event of an accident or emergency, the guard will give the appropriate directions and instructions. There are safety notices posted throughout the train, which the public address system will routinely invite you to consult.

The train generally offers good comfort too, with well designed, supportive seats – and the option to stretch your legs. However, it is not unknown for the air conditioning to fail in the summer. If that happens, the guard will open emergency windows, which will result in a noisier journey, but a less overheated one.

Facilities at stations

Aberdeen, Elgin, and Inverness are staffed; and Inverurie, Huntly, Keith, Forres and Nairn are staffed part-time. Dyce and Insch are unstaffed.

Without exception, all advertised trains stop at all eight intermediate stations between Aberdeen and Inverness. ScotRail's 'Inverness to Aberdeen' pocket timetable lists in some detail the facilities at each station. These are summarised as follows:

- cycle racks/storage: all stations.
- car parking: all stations (parking charges apply at Aberdeen and Inverness).
- taxi ranks: all stations, except Insch, Huntly and Keith.
- ScotRail pre-booking 'Cab&Go' taxi service: Dyce, Elgin, Huntly, and Inverurie.
- ticket vending machines: all stations.
- toilets: all stations, except Dyce and Insch (at some stations the key may be required from the ticket office).
- refreshment facilities: Aberdeen, Inverurie (Coco Works), Nairn (The Coffee Station) and Inverness. The Union Square shopping mall in Aberdeen offers a range of eating places and is linked directly to the station.

Buildings of architectural or historic interest

There is much architectural and historical interest along the line, including structures which survive from the days of the Great North of Scotland and Highland Railway Companies. These include many bridges, some of which are noted in 'The view from your window' (*see next chapter*), but most obvious to train passengers are lineside buildings.

The Scottish Government agency, Historic Environment Scotland, has 'listed' no fewer than 17 railway structures of 'special' architectural or historical interest on the line:

- One is 'Category A', i.e. 'buildings of national or international importance, either architectural or historic; or fine, little-altered examples of some particular period, style or building type'.
- 14 are 'Category B', i.e. 'buildings of regional or more than local importance; or major examples of some particular period, style or building type, which may have been altered'.
- Two are 'Category C', i.e. 'buildings of local importance; lesser examples of any period, style or building type, as originally constructed or moderately altered; and simple, traditional buildings that group well with other listed buildings'.

The locations (B-listed unless otherwise stated) are:

- Aberdeen station and road overbridge (A-listed)
- a former suburban railway ticket office at the corner of Guild Street and College Street, immediately above Aberdeen station
- Inverurie station building
- former Inverurie Locomotive Works
- station building and footbridge at Insch
- three bridges over the railway north of Kennethmont, within the policies of Leith Hall
- viaduct over the River Deveron near Rothiemay
- former station at Mulben

- Boat o' Brig railway bridge over the River Spey between Keith and Elgin
- former GNSR station at Elgin East
- former GNSR 'Elgin Centre' signal box at Elgin East (C-listed)
- former GNSR engine shed at Elgin East (C-listed)
- viaduct over the River Findhorn, west of Forres
- viaduct over the River Nairn
- station buildings on both platforms at Nairn
- two signal boxes and overbridge at Nairn station
- a former railway dwelling adjacent to Nairn station

On your journey you may also spot some other buildings dating back to past eras of the railway. Keep your eyes peeled.

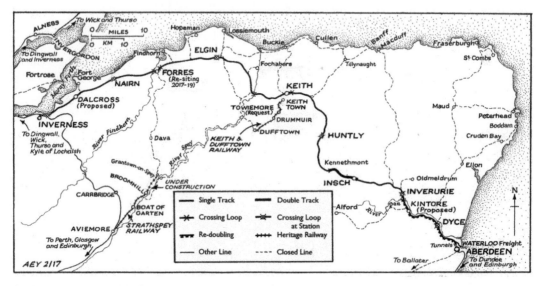

The dramatic shrinkage of the former Great North of Scotland Railway network is demonstrated by Alan Young's hand-drawn map of today's railway, with only one operational branch line (for freight from Aberdeen Waterloo) still connecting to the Aberdeen-Inverness route. *Alan Young*

CHAPTER FOUR

The view from your window

Aberdeen: The Granite City

Aberdeen is Scotland's third-largest city, with a population of around 200,000. Its older buildings are constructed predominately from local granite, which can appear grey and drab in bad weather but which sparkle in the sunshine. Hence, the city is often also referred to as 'The Grey City' and 'The Silver City' (depending on the weather). The city's development was based on fishing, associated fish curing, processing and freezing, ship building, paper making, and textiles.

Today, however, despite the recent downturn, it is a thriving and vibrant 'Oil Capital', having been the centre of North Sea oil management and services since 1970. Aberdeen boasts two universities: the University of Aberdeen (founded 1495) and Robert Gordon's University (awarded university status in 1992).

The city is served by four rail companies. Abellio ScotRail operates trains south to Dundee, Perth, Edinburgh, and Glasgow, and north to Inverness; Virgin Trains run daytime services to London King's Cross via the East Coast; Serco runs the overnight Caledonian Sleeper service to London Euston via the West Coast; and Cross Country operates the longest unbroken journey in the United Kingdom from

Aberdeen to Penzance, which departs every morning at 08.20 and arrives at its Cornish destination 13 hours and 23 minutes later.

The present-day Aberdeen station dates from 1867, although it was rebuilt due to increasing congestion in the years before World War One. The platforms were covered by canopies for weather protection, and were raised in height because the original low ones were considered dangerous. They became slippy due to a build-up of slime from the large number of fish trains passing through! The outbreak of war interrupted progress and the new station was not completed until 1920. Further alterations and modifications (including the removal of the north bay platforms by 1971 and the replacement of the booking office with new Travel Centres in 1978 and 2007) have been made over subsequent years, but it is essentially the same old 'Joint Station', although the frontage is now part of the Union Square retail development.

In 1891 the Great North of Scotland Railway Company decided to enter the hotel business and purchased and renovated the substantial Palace Hotel on Union Street. A new covered footbridge, accessed by hydraulic lifts, connected the hotel directly to the station. When the Great North introduced summer day excursions from Aberdeen to Boat of Garten in 1905, passengers could pre-order 'cold luncheon' and 'teas' in advance and these were supplied by the hotel. On 30 October 1941 it was destroyed by a fire in which six chambermaids lost their lives.

The Company opened the plush Cruden Bay Hotel and golf course south of Peterhead in 1899, but it always struggled due to its relative remoteness and short summer season. It was requisitioned by the Government in 1939, never re-opened, and was demolished in the post-War years. In 1910 the company acquired the Station Hotel adjoining Aberdeen station and, although now privately owned, it is still serving rail passengers today.

A4 Pacific No. 60009 *Union of South Africa* passes Union Terrace Gardens in Aberdeen, hauling the Inverness-Edinburgh leg of the Great Britain VII tour train on 3 May 2014. The railway here was formerly four tracks wide, but land has now been lost to a 'relief' road. *Keith Jones*

Exploring Aberdeen

Aberdeen's main thoroughfare and shopping street is Union Street, named after the Act of Union between Great Britain and Ireland of 1801. There are the modern St Nicholas and Bon Accord shopping malls between Union Street and George Street, and the Union Square complex next to the station. The Tourist Information Centre on the corner of Union Street and Shiprow (at the Castlegate end) is open all year and is adjacent to the Maritime Museum and Provost Ross House.

The museum reflects the city's past in relation to fishing, shipping and oil, and entry is free. The Aberdeen Art Gallery in Schoolhill is currently under redevelopment and will re-open in early 2018. The magnificent architecture of the University's former Marischal College in Broad Street (home of Aberdeen City Council since 2011) is worth viewing, and a walk through the cobbled streets of Old Aberdeen, with King's College as its centrepiece, is rewarding.

Aberdeen is the port of departure for Orkney and Shetland, with overnight car/passenger ferries operating seven nights per week. The large, modern vessels are operated by Northlink to Kirkwall and Lerwick and depart from the terminal on Jamieson's Quay, just over five minutes' walk from the railway station.

Aberdeen to Dyce

Trains for Inverness normally depart from Platforms 6 or 7 of this A-listed station. These are the two through platforms – among the longest in Scotland - seen directly through the main ticket barrier, although Platform 7 has to be accessed via the signed overbridge. Both platform ends are designated and signposted

The distinctive 'saw-tooth' pitched roof design of the Carriage & Wagon Shop of the former Inverurie Locomotive Works now protects smart town apartments, the Garioch Heritage Society and a cafe in the B-listed structure, seen on 19 April 2017. *David Fasken*

North (N) and South (S). The trains for Inverness can depart from either end, but the location is clearly indicated on the departure board in the station concourse.

As the train departs, it passes the former steam locomotive turntable on your immediate left, before traversing Union Terrace Gardens, the subject of debate in recent years over its future development, with His Majesty's Theatre above. The line begins a 1 in 72 climb up the Denburn Valley via two tunnels, Schoolhill (236 yards) and Hutcheon Street (270 yards), to the site of the original terminus at Kittybrewster. From 2019 the current single-track line will become double again from this point to Inverurie.

On your right is the branch to the line's terminus from 1856 to 1867 at the harbour at Waterloo, still used for freight today. Although Kittybrewster lost its terminus status to Waterloo and 'Joint Station' and its Works to Inverurie, it continued to function as an important locomotive depot, goods marshalling yard, and station until the 1960s. Today, little remains.

When the first section of the railway opened from Kittybrewster to Huntly in 1854, the Electric Telegraph Company connected all stations by telegraph. The Great North was far ahead of other British railway companies in this respect. The Aberdeen to Inverness railway today remains the last route to be connected by telegraph for communication between signal boxes. The poles which line much of the route are still in operation.

Kittybrewster was the scene of a tragic accident on only the third day of operation. On 23 September 1854 an incoming train from Huntly, attempting to make up time following delay, failed to slow on greasy rails and the reverse gear slipped into forward position unnoticed by the inexperienced driver. The locomotive ran into a line of stationary coaches in the platform, destroying the leading carriage, killing a lady passenger, and severely injuring several others. It was not an auspicious start to train operations.

The B-listed Insch signal box dates from 1880 and remains fully functional, controlling the start of the six-mile double-track section to Kennethmont, the single track towards Inverurie and the B9002 road crossing. *Merrill MacWilliam (from a photo by David Fasken)*

A feature of historical note was the introduction in the 1880s of suburban trains between Aberdeen and Dyce. There were intermediate stations at Schoolhill, Hutcheon Street, Kittybrewster, Don Street, Woodside, Persley, Bucksburn, Bankhead, and Stoneywood (*see map insert on page v*). By 1887 eight trains ran daily in each direction and, initially, they were known as the 'Jubilees' as their introduction coincided with Queen Victoria's 50th year on the throne.

However, these popular trains soon became referred to by regular travellers as the 'subbies', and by the 1890s the number of trains had increased to 20 daily in each direction. They were used by large numbers travelling to and from work, especially for the many papermills on the River Don, such as at Mugiemoss and Stoneywood. The 'subbies' eventually succumbed to the problem of aging rolling stock in the face of increasing competition from buses and trams, and all Aberdeen's suburban services were withdrawn in 1937. The intermediate stations between Aberdeen and Dyce closed, with the exception of Bucksburn and Kittybrewster, which survived until 1956 and 1968 respectively.

Dyce: Aberdeen International Airport

Dyce was a satellite town of Aberdeen. Its station closed in 1968, but massive industrial and housing expansion associated with the developing North Sea oil industry saw it re-open in 1984. Dyce station became, for a time, the most-used unstaffed station in Scotland. As your train enters the station there are good views on the left to Aberdeen International Airport, including the heliport, one of the busiest in the world, from where oil rigs are serviced. Many oilmen use the station to transfer to and from the Airport on their way on and off-shore. There is a connecting taxi service.

The level crossing barrier is closed to the B9002 road on 24 March 2017 as the 12.00 train from Aberdeen awaits departure from Insch station, while the 10.57 from Inverness approaches the southbound platform. Both trains are Class 170s, most of which will be displaced from the route in 2018-19 when refurbished 'High Speed Trains' dating from the late 1970s will provide extra capacity on this increasingly busy line. *David Fasken*

On the right-hand side, the high signal box at the south end still controls the main line, and until 1979 it served the junction with the Buchan Line to Fraserburgh and Peterhead (although the section from Maud to Peterhead had closed in 1970). Considerable fish traffic from these two ports headed for southern markets via Dyce and the main line to Aberdeen. Itinerant fish workers following the shoals of 'silver darlings' (herring) also travelled south by train to English fishing ports such as Great Yarmouth. Today the trackbed of the line forms the Formartine and Buchan Way for walkers and cyclists: 23 miles to Maud and a further 15 to Fraserburgh and 13 to Peterhead. The trackbed is protected from development so that the railway can be reinstated in the future, and studies are underway in respect of the 13 miles to Ellon, which has expanded in recent years as a major commuter feed to the city.

The station building serving the Buchan Line was used for a fish and chip shop and after-school club until destroyed by fire in 2015, but has since been rebuilt. In 2016 a new passenger overbridge with lifts was installed at the north end of the platforms, replacing the old iron lattice footbridge.

Dyce to Inverurie

With the train accelerating out of the crossing loop you will see, on the left-hand side, the new freight depot at Raith's Farm, a strange name for a modern rail facility. Self-contained within its own compound it has been used in recent times for the movement of oil pipes. The railway now runs under the new Aberdeen Western Peripheral Route which will be completed in 2018. The train then follows the course of the River Don on the right-hand side, largely on the route of the former Aberdeenshire Canal.

On 1 May 2014, A4 Pacific No. 60009 *Union of South Africa* races past Ardmore Distillery at Kennethmont towards the single-track section through the policies of Leith Hall mansion. The locomotive is hauling the Aberdeen-Inverness leg of the Great Britain VII tour train. The signal box in the photograph (beyond which is the former station building) controls the entry to and exit from the six-mile double-track section from Insch, and the single-track towards Huntly. *David Fasken*

The high peaks of Bennachie appear for the first time, also on the right of the train, and these distinctive hilltops dominate the skyline for a considerable distance before and beyond Inverurie. There were three intermediate stops on this stretch of line at Pitmedden, Kinaldie and Kintore, but they all succumbed to the 'Beeching Axe' in 1964. Kintore was the former junction for the 16-mile line to Alford. There is a proposal to re-build and re-open this station following significant housing expansion in the town, although this has been talked about for nearly 40 years!

The former Inverurie Paper Mill soon hoves into view on the right-hand side. Established in 1852 by the Tait family whose connection with Port Elphinstone dates back to the 1650s, it closed its doors for the last time in 2009 after succumbing to cheap international competition. Esparto grass for conversion to paper was delivered at one time by train via a dedicated siding off the main line and, until the 1970s, a hand-propelled narrow gauge railway system operated within the plant to convey paper to the 'rippers', which cut large paper rolls to marketable sizes.

As the train approaches Inverurie, you will see on the left-hand side evidence of the old Aberdeenshire Canal. The canal opened in 1805 and ran from sea level at Aberdeen Harbour to a height of 168 feet at Port Elphinstone (named after Sir Robert Elphinstone who supported its construction) one mile east of Inverurie. Height was gained by three flights of locks (totalling 17) at Kittybrewster, Stoneywood and Kintore. Both passengers and goods were conveyed, but it took three hours to navigate 17 miles from Inverurie to Kittybrewster and, consequently, the service seldom worked the final locks to the harbour and terminated near Woodside, two miles from the city. Service was frequently suspended in winter due to ice. Goods carried were mainly granite from local quarries, fertiliser, and farm produce.

Financial problems, diminishing traffic, and the impending arrival of the railway led to the sale of the canal to the Great North of Scotland Railway Company in 1845. The lawyers tasked with the conveyancing of the

The B-listed lattice girder bridge carrying the railway over the River Deveron at Rothiemay (between Huntly and Keith) is seen here, looking south, on 14 September 2013. The original single-track stone crossing was built a few yards downstream (to the left) and was replaced in 1900 by today's bridge when the line was subject to a 'deviation' to accommodate double-track. *David Spaven*

Today, the station is staffed and the original, now B-listed, building incorporates a comfortable, wood-panelled, and tastefully restored and decorated waiting room. Also within the building there is a privately-run coffee shop called 'Coco Works' which, in the early 20th century, was a private waiting room for the Earl of Kintore. On the main platform beneath the canopy, you can see the original station clock, the old platform weigh-scales, and the wall-mounted, decorative cast-iron water fountain. Outside opening hours, there is a draughty shelter incorporating a ticket vending machine.

As the train departs, the former buildings, also B-listed, of the renowned Inverurie Locomotive Works can be viewed to the left. The Great North built their original works in 1854 at the Aberdeen terminus of Kittybrewster. By the late 19th century these had become cramped and inadequate. The company decided to relocate to a new 24-acre site, of which six acres were covered, at Inverurie. The new Works incorporated a comprehensive range of technical facilities, serving Locomotive, Carriage & Wagon, and Permanent Way departments. It had its own electricity generating plant from the start, which continued in use until the 1950s.

The new Works resulted in a huge increase in the town's population (estimated at an additional 1,200) and the Company built houses nearby for their employees, with electric power supplied from the Works. A distinctive development of some 160 dwellings became known as 'The Colony' and can be glimpsed through the industrial and retail development on your left. Inverurie Locomotive Works only built ten locomotives, the main function being repairs, rebuilds, and carriage construction. From the 1920s the company's motor buses were serviced. The plant operated on a 24-hour basis throughout both World Wars and, at its peak, employed a workforce of 850 people.

As steam gave way to diesel in the 1950s and 1960s, the Works adapted and remained busy, servicing diesel locomotives and multiple units. But investment eventually dwindled and, in British Railways days,

Extensive forests and woodlands surround the central section of the Aberdeen-Inverness line. Timber was conveyed by train from Huntly freight depot to southern markets in the late 1990s and early 2000s. On 3 May 2017, a Class 158 is entering Strathbogie, heading for Gartly and Huntly, with the 10.13 Aberdeen-Inverness train. *David Fasken*

Inverurie was considered too isolated from the main British rail system to the south. The Works siren hooted for the last time on 31 December 1969, and Inverurie was consigned to history as a railway town. Today, some buildings have been renovated and converted into modern apartments. The distinctive 'saw-tooth' pitched roof design remains. The Colony houses are now privately owned.

The remaining link to Inverurie's historical railway connections lies with its football club, Inverurie Loco. Works FC, founded by Great North of Scotland Railway workers in 1902, and who today compete at Senior level in the Scottish Highland Football League. They still play at their original ground which was part of the Works site. You can see clearly to the left the ground and floodlights of Harlaw Park as the train accelerates from the station.

To your right, the 1902 wooden signal box still operates. It originally controlled main line traffic, the short branch from Inverurie to Oldmeldrum (closed 1965), and the approaches to the Works. With 96 levers, it was the second largest box on the Great North system.

Inverurie to Insch

The Great North was an innovative company. From 1886, in order to facilitate the handling of mail, it introduced a sorting carriage between Aberdeen and Keith, and it pioneered lineside apparatus for receiving and delivering mail bags 'on the move'. Pitcaple, Oyne, Kennethmont (between Insch and Huntly) and Rothiemay (between Huntly and Keith) were intermediate stations with such facilities. The sorting carriage was withdrawn in May 1916 as a wartime economy and was never reinstated.

Wardhouse station, near the summit of the Aberdeen-Inverness line between Insch and Kennethmont, was originally built for the Gordon family of the local estate of the same name. Serving few people, it closed as early as 1961, and today stands neglected and semi-derelict. *Merrill MacWilliam (from a photo by David Fasken)*

Interestingly, the company's blacksmith James Duncan used the same exchange principle, combined with textile technology, to introduce the automatic collection and delivery of the physical 'token' allowing one train to enter single-track sections. From 1889 this enabled trains moving at speeds of up to 50 mph to exchange tokens. The Great North's innovative approach placed it well ahead of other railway companies.

The keen-eyed passenger will notice a 40-foot stone monument over the cusp of a small rise to the right of the train as it leaves Inverurie. This is a memorial to the Battle of Harlaw fought on this site on 24 July 1411. It was constructed by the Burgh of Aberdeen in 1911 to commemorate the 500th anniversary. The battle was the result of a power struggle between the barons of the west coast and north-east Scotland over control of the Earldom of Ross in the Highlands. Donald, Lord of the Isles, advanced with 10,000 clansmen on Aberdeen, and at Harlaw he confronted the Earl of Mar and his 1,500 or so local gentry. The result was indecisive, with over 1,400 lives lost, although the Earl of Mar forced Donald to retreat and the Earl claimed the moral victory. The fighting was so bloody and fierce that the battle is often referred to as 'Red Harlaw'.

On the approach to Inveramsay, a former junction station, the train passes under the new road bridge completed in 2016 to alleviate road congestion on the main A96 at the notorious one-way under-bridge controlled by traffic lights. Inveramsay was the junction for the line north to Turriff and Macduff and you can see its remains on the right-hand side. It closed to passengers as early as 1951. Freight continued until the 1960s.

Now clearly visible on the left side of the train is the distinctive hill of Bennachie with its two main 'summits' of Mither Tap and Oxen Craig (the higher at 1,733 feet). The hill is popular with walkers, joggers and cyclists and the views from the Iron Age fort at the top are far-reaching and impressive. There is a Visitor Centre on the east side providing a range of information and activities.

Huntly signal box basks in sunshine on 3 May 2017 during a pause between trains. The box is situated at the south end of the station's crossing loop, above the A96 trunk road, and also controls the connection to the mothballed sidings in the former freight depot. *David Fasken*

The train runs through rich agricultural land with the large white mansion of Logie House on the right. It was originally a fortified castle tower built in the 1670s, although its 7,500 acre estate dated back to 1492. The house was devastated by fire in 1975, but was restored in 2009 as a 13-bedroom venue for weddings and functions. The estate is now much reduced in size to 130 acres.

Below the peaks of Bennachie the train passes Pitcaple and Oyne (both stations closed in 1968). On the left you will observe the 17th-century pink-washed, solid granite Z-plan tower of Harthill Castle which was the ancient seat of the family of Leith of Harthill. Originally built in the 15th century, it was restored in 1638, but subsequently lay in ruins for over 300 years until rebuilt between 1975 and 1977 and winning the prestigious Saltire Award. It is a Grade-A listed building.

Insch: A traditional country station

As Bennachie recedes, the train approaches Insch, a small, popular, country town. Originally an agricultural centre, in recent times it has expanded considerably with modern housing. Many people commute daily into Aberdeen by train, bus or car. The station is unstaffed. The wooden station building and footbridge (both B-listed), and signal box (on the right at the west end) are particularly striking, as they date from 1880 and evoke a feeling of being transported back in time. At the rear of the western (Inverness-bound) platform you can see the cables which operate the semaphore signals on the approach to the station, a traditional method which will disappear in time.

In 1992, following years of negligible maintenance and infestation of both dry and wet rot, ScotRail proposed to demolish the main four-room building and reached the stage of commencing the tender

Letting off steam! A4 Pacific No. 60009 *Union of South Africa* gives herself away on 1 May 2014 as she departs from Huntly towards Pirriesmill, heading for a water stop at Keith before proceeding on to Inverness with the Great Britain VII tour train. *David Fasken*

exercise. Unfortunately the building was not listed. Insch Community Enterprise, supported by Gordon District Council, came to the rescue. European Union Funding in 1995 contributed half the cost of renovation and the building re-opened in 1997 as Insch Connection Museum. It is a rare example of traditional rural railway architecture. The Museum reflects all aspects of local life and today is open every Wednesday and Sunday afternoon from 13.30 to 17.00 from April to October inclusive. Other groups and school parties can visit by special arrangement. (*See Chapter 5 for contact details*).

On the hill above the railway to the right, you can see the remains of the castle of Dunnideer, a medieval tower house dating from around 1260. It was built on the site of an existing vitrified hill fort from 250BC. It was a single rectangular tower, and is believed to have contained several levels. On the lower slopes of Dunnideer Hill you will see the golf course. Although Insch Golf Club recently celebrated its centenary, today's golf course was completed in 1997 and a new clubhouse added as recently as 2004. The course's development was not helped by its requisition in 1940 for use as a grenade range by the Army.

Insch to Huntly

As the train leaves Insch it is running on the only remaining double-track section on the entire line, and climbs steadily for five miles to its summit at 594 feet between Wardhouse (closed 1961) and Kennethmont (closed 1968). The station at Wardhouse was built for the Gordon family who owned the nearby Wardhouse Estate. Shortly before the train arrives at the former station of Kennethmont (on your left, recently re-painted in railway colours), you can see Leith Hall mansion ahead and on the right. The signal box here (on your right) controls the return to single-track working.

Class 25 locomotive No. 25234 shunts bulk whisky containers at the 18 September 1976 opening ceremony for a new rail-connected storage terminal built by Chivas in and around the former GNSR engine shed at Keith. This was the last location in the north of Scotland to send bulk spirit by rail to Central Belt maturation plants, in 1992. However, there are hopes that the Keith terminal and a mothballed rail freight depot at Elgin will once again see whisky moving by train. *Stuart Sellar*

Also, on the left, is Ardmore Distillery which was built in 1898 by Adam Teacher, the son of William Teacher. The distillery produces a peated single malt taking water from the nearby 1,500-feet Knockando Hill. It has eight stills, and until as late as 2001 it used coal to fire them. It had its own maltings until the mid-1970s and its own cooperage until the late-1980s. The railway played a big part in the development of the business, and you may spot an abandoned private siding still connected to the main line. Today, the distillery is owned by Beam Suntory, an American subsidiary of Suntory of Japan.

As the train again enters single track you may catch another, albeit fleeting, glimpse of Leith Hall mansion house to your right. This is more likely in winter when the leaves are off the trees. Leith Hall was the ancestral home to ten generations of the same family, 'Leith' later 'Leith-Hay', for over 300 years. It was built in 1650 and passed into the care of the National Trust for Scotland in 1945 after the death of the last Laird in a motorcycle accident. The house is reputedly haunted by, among others, the fourth Laird John Leith III who died from gunshot wounds in 1763 after a quarrel in an Aberdeen tavern. Today, the house is open to the public at weekends from Easter to the end of October and additionally on Thursday and Friday in July, August and September. Visits are by guided tour only and there is a tearoom and shop. The gardens and estate walks are open all year.

The railway line runs through the Leith Hall estate, and the house is linked directly to Kennethmont station by a carriageway built when the line opened in 1854. It crosses the line via an ornamental and ballustraded B-listed overbridge designed by the Great North's engineer Alexander Gibb, who trained under Thomas Telford and Robert Stevenson.

As the train emerges into Strathbogie, you will glimpse the imposing Iron Age hilltop fort of Tap o' Noth to your left, close to the village of Rhynie. It is the second-largest such fort in Scotland and there is a good footpath to the summit at 1,851 feet, from where you can view the impressive remains and enjoy splendid

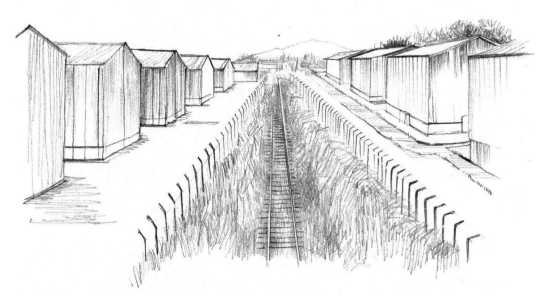

Train travellers pass through a distinctive man-made landscape west of Keith, flanked by the Chivas Regal bonded warehouses, where Scotch whisky must, by statute, be matured in barrels for a minimum of three years. *Merrill MacWilliam (from a photo by David Spaven)*

In August 1907, local school children lined the route from Kennethmont Station – including this ballustraded bridge carrying the Leith Hall driveway over the railway – to welcome home the Laird, Charles Leith-Hay, and his new bride, Henrietta O'Neill, from their honeymoon. The couple had arrived on the GNSR's Royal Train, normally used to transport the Royal Family over the 'Deeside Line' from Aberdeen to Ballater. *Merrill MacWilliam (from a photo by Graham Nealgrove)*

transaction dragged their feet to such an extent that the sale was not complete when railway construction commenced east of Inverurie in 1853. The contractors, faced with a further delay following severe winter weather, proceeded to breach the canal bank near Kintore leaving several barges stranded between there and Stoneywood. Temporary repairs were effected, but the incident forced the lawyers into action. It is unclear whether the Great North Directors connived in or even inspired this turn of events; but the reputation of the railway company was damaged locally long before a locomotive wheel had turned. Much of the route of the railway line on which you are travelling today was built on the bed of the Aberdeenshire Canal.

Inverurie: Heart of the Garioch

Until the railway Works arrived at the turn of the 19th and 20th centuries, the town of Inverurie was essentially an agricultural centre serving the hinterland locally known as 'The Garioch'. The town is built on the confluence of the Rivers Don and Ury, and its distinctive triangular town centre is dominated by the grand Town Hall built in 1862 (whose 'pagoda' clock tower can be seen from the train to the left). While the town grew, and changed following the construction of the railway Works, the last 40 years have seen massive expansion directly linked to the development of North Sea oil.

The station at which you arrive was opened in 1902. It replaced the original small station half a mile to the south, and was much closer to the adjoining Locomotive Works constructed at the same time (1898 – 1905). Originally, this was a three-platform junction station (for the short branch to Oldmeldrum), but the bay platform on the north side has disappeared within the boundaries of the neighbouring garden centre on your right.

The last passenger charter train to visit the erstwhile Dufftown terminus of the former Keith-Craigellachie-Elgin cross-country route. A Class 47 loco and coaches in BR InterCity livery prepare to return south on 24 March 1991, overlooked by the silo which, for two decades from the mid-1960s, had handled barley for the whisky industry, brought in by train from eastern England. *Bill Roberton*

and is open all year. The approach is via an attractive tree-lined avenue, off which are the sporting grounds of the local football, cricket and golf clubs as well as the more recent Nordic Ski Centre.

Huntly to Keith

Four miles on from Huntly, the railway crosses the River Deveron by means of a substantial lattice girder bridge, now B-listed. The original single-track stone crossing was built a few yards downstream, and was replaced in 1900 by today's bridge when the line was subject to a 'deviation' to allow for double-track. The masonry structure stood unused alongside and was not demolished until 1979. Its foundations can still be seen today, downstream from the right-hand side of the train.

As the Deveron and the former Rothiemay station (closed 1968) are left behind to be replaced by the River Isla, the train rushes through the sites of two former stations, Cairnie Junction and Grange, both of which served the 'Coast Line' to Elgin via Buckie which branched here to the north. The two stations were only half a mile apart, and both closed in 1968 along with the entire 'Coast Line'. Away to the right you will spot the distinctive and round-topped Knock Hill below which, to the east, ran the railway. Soon, as the train leaves Aberdeenshire and enters Moray, the wooded hill of 'The Balloch' appears to your left. Here, there are good tracks for walking, and the open moorland at the summit of Meikle Balloch (1,200 feet) affords spectacular views of the surrounding countryside.

As the train approaches Keith it enters a long crossing loop on the east side of the town. This is now the only loop on the Aberdeen – Inverness railway which is situated outside a station, and passengers can be forgiven for thinking they have become stuck in the middle of nowhere as trains are often scheduled to

On 13 September 2013, a DB Schenker Class 66 locomotive shunts empty tank containers in Elgin freight depot, ready for the next day's inaugural run of the 'Lifting the Spirit' trial train service to Grangemouth. Life-expired timber wagons are returning to nature in the background, while the tank containers are flanked on the left by the neglected rear of the otherwise imposing former Elgin East passenger station. *David Spaven*

idle here for several minutes while waiting to cross. From the loop, on the right-hand side, there are views over the valley to the small village of Newmill. From here James Gordon-Bennett (born 1795) emigrated to the United States to follow a journalistic career. He founded the *New York Herald* in 1835. His son, James Gordon-Bennett Junior (born 1841), ultimately inherited a newspaper empire and great wealth and led an extravagant and wild lifestyle, often full of society scandal. This gave birth to the popular exclamation of surprise: 'Gordon Bennett!'.

The piles of barrels in the yards on the approach to the right signify the importance of whisky to Keith. The former railway locomotive depot to your left was converted in 1976 into a directly rail-connected bulk spirit storage facility for Chivas Brothers. Rail traffic ceased in 1992, but there are hopes that a future switch from road haulage for Speyside whisky flows to Central Scotland maturation and bottling plants will allow this facility – and/or the mothballed Keith freight depot nearby – to be again served by trains.

Keith: Whisky Capital

Keith station was, until the 1980s, called 'Keith Junction' because the Great North's alternative 'Glen Route' to Elgin via Dufftown and Craigellachie branched off here. The Dufftown platform can be seen on the left and is still used for the occasional train, including the luxury tourist 'Royal Scotsman' which is stabled overnight to allow visits to local distilleries. The line to Dufftown survived the Beeching era, as it served barley silos for the whisky industry until the early 1980s and, from 1984, was used by the 'Northern Belle', a summer excursion train from Aberdeen operated by local businessman John Begg. Special trains from as

The wood-panelled and stained-glass former booking hall of Elgin East station in April 2017. Built in 1902 with a high-vaulted roof, the hall is flanked today by several offices and businesses. What might it have looked like if the passenger trains had not been withdrawn in 1968, and subsequent inevitable 'modernisation' had been imposed? *David Spaven*

far south as London also used the line, but rising costs and deteriorating infrastructure saw the last 'special' operate in March 1991. The line was then closed. Another beautiful railway line was in danger of being lost.

However, two years later a private group, the Keith & Dufftown Railway Association, purchased the line from British Rail for £11 (£1 a mile). Although the connection was severed at Keith Junction in 1998, trains recommenced between Dufftown and Drummuir in 2000 and over the entire line to Keith Town station the following year. Towiemore, which served the former adjacent distillery, closed in 1968 but was re-opened as a request stop in 2016.

Today 'The Whisky Line' is Britain's most northerly heritage railway and is run entirely by volunteers. Its long-term objective is to re-gain entry into Keith Junction and thereafter to reconnect to the British railway system. In 2017, encouraging discussions were held with ScotRail and the Scottish Government. Today, there are three return journeys between the two towns on Saturdays and Sundays from Easter to the end of September; with additional Friday services in June, July, and August. Throughout the season there are a number of 'Special Events' including Childrens' Easter Egg Hunt, Speyside Whisky Festivals, Pie & Pint Night, 1940s Weekend, and Halloween Ghost Train. (*See Chapter Five for contact details*).

Keith to Elgin

When the train leaves Keith it passes between the bonded warehouses of Chivas Brothers on both sides of the track. Millions of pounds worth of whisky is maturing, some lying in excess of 20 years before despatch. The company's most famous brand is its luxury blend Chivas Regal which it launched for the American market in the early years of the 20th century.

No chance of a day return to Buckie in April 2017, but the trademark iron barriers at the former ticket hatches stylishly complement the fine wood and plaster work of the former GNSR booking hall at Elgin East. *David Spaven*

Malt whisky, which contributes to the Chivas Regal blend of malt and grain whiskies, is produced at the town's Strathisla Distillery, a stone's throw from the railway station. Chivas Regal itself is blended and bottled in Central Scotland. Founded in 1786, Strathisla is the oldest Highland distillery and was acquired by Chivas in 1950, having supplied single malt for Regal for many years before that. Today, the company is owned by Pernod Ricard, and over 36 million litres are exported annually all over the world. The bonds which you are passing were originally of wooden construction, but some of the roofs collapsed during the severe snowstorms of 2010 and have been rebuilt with modern steel cladding.

The present-day Chivas Bond No. 1 (the first warehouse on the right) was the site of a secret and little-known factory constructed in 1938–39 for the war effort. Officially the Tarmore Factory, but referred to locally as 'The Hush Hush', it was a gas factory built by the Air Ministry, administered by RAF Kinloss and operated by the British Oxygen Company (BOC). It produced hydrogen, oxygen and later nitrogen. It was located here due to water availability (for production and fire safety), proximity to the RAF base and the railway, and concealment from the enemy. Electricity was supplied from Loch Tummel hydro plant in Perthshire by overhead line and huge batteries within the plant ensured a regular supply.

The hydrogen was used for inflating defensive barrage balloons around the UK. Wagons transporting the gas cylinders were moved by the shunting locomotive serving the nearby Aultmore Distillery although, as production increased, a dedicated engine appeared. Up to 40 local people were employed and everyone involved had to sign the Official Secrets Act. Some military personnel were stationed on the site. After the war BOC produced nitrogen but the plant was uncompetitive and closed in 1955. It was sold to Chivas two years later.

Four miles west of Keith, the train passes Glentauchers Distillery on your left. It was built in 1897 by a Glasgow whisky trader W.P. Lowrie in partnership with the blender James Buchanan. Today, there are six

Memories of the nationwide network of railway station bookstalls and the past popularity of smoking at the former Elgin East station in April 2017.

stills and, although mothballed from 1985 to 1992, it has been owned by Chivas Brothers since 2005 and currently produces 3.4 million litres annually. Until 1964 it had its own goods siding and private platform for the distillery workers.

After the B-listed Mulben station (closed 1964), the train descends the steep wooded valley of the Burn of Mulben at 1 in 60 and emerges at speed on the steel bridge crossing one of Scotland's famous salmon fishing rivers: the Spey. This is the B-listed Boat o' Brig and to the left is the road crossing. There was a medieval bridge here and its tolls supported a local hospital. After being destroyed by flood it was replaced by a ferry until a new suspension bridge was constructed by Captain Samuel Brown RN in 1830. Its tollhouse survives, tucked into the hill on the east side of the river.

Today's modern road bridge, a single arch-topped steel truss, was put in place in 1952 and allows only single-file traffic. The railway viaduct over which your train crosses is a steel-lattice girder bridge built by the Highland Railway in 1906 to replace Joseph Mitchell's original plate-girder construction of 1858. At one time, timber from the forests around Aviemore and Aberlour was floated down the River Spey to supply a thriving ship-building industry at Garmouth and Kingston at the river mouth.

The train accelerates to climb the 1 in 100 west side of the Spey Valley and, if you look closely to the left as Boat o' Brig falls behind, you will see the remains of the three-and-a-half mile railway from Orton to Rothes. This was part of the Morayshire Railway from Lossiemouth to Elgin and on to Rothes using the Highland Railway's line from Elgin to Orton. The Orton – Rothes line opened in 1858 but, when the Morayshire opened its direct route to Rothes south from Elgin via Longmorn in 1862, this link quickly became redundant. It was closed to regular traffic as early as 1866, although the track was not lifted until 1907.

High-capacity hopper wagons – which had conveyed barley from eastern England – await discharge at the whisky maltings at the terminus of the Burghead branch line on 9 May 1991. Regular freight train services for the whisky industry in the north of Scotland ceased in 1992 as a result of road haulage competition, and much of the barley for the industry is now sourced from within Scotland. *Bill Roberton*

The former Orton and Orbliston stations, both closed in 1964 and now private residences, are passed in quick succession on your right-hand side. Orbliston was the junction for the Highland Railway's three mile branch to Fochabers which closed to passengers as early as 1931 and to freight in 1966. The station was called Fochabers Town which was rather a misnomer because it was situated a good half-mile from the town on the west side of the Spey to avoid a costly river crossing (opposite the modern-day Baxters canning factory). Some remains of this line can be seen on the right past Orbliston Station.

The Fochabers branch was used by the family of the Duke of Richmond and Gordon to travel to and from the family seat of Gordon Castle near Fochabers. Alfred Forbes recalled an incident at Orbliston station in 1923 while working as a young railwayman:

'The Duke's two daughters, the Duchess of Northumberland and Lady Violet Brassey, were changing trains on their way home. One of the ladies had, under her arm, a small Pekinese dog for which a train ticket was required. So was a degree of diplomacy on the part of the railwayman: 'I knew instinctively that I did not address them as we did ordinary people, "wifie" for the local women, or "missus" for strangers. Trotting beside them, I repeated "Please ma'am! Sevenpence for the dog" but they ignored me completely.... Entranced as I was, my duty was clear, the money must be obtained.

We were now approaching the little branch train, with its one coach, only one compartment of which was marked "First Class". I threw myself before the door, and extended my arms to full width, and demanded in clear tones: "Please ma'am, sevenpence for the dog – or I can't let you go in the train". There was an astonished pause, and then a stare of Medusa-like intensity, and a hand was drawn across my face, not a blow and certainly not a caress, and then a voice compounded of shock and wrath, such as I have never since heard: "Get out of my way, you little bastard".'

Now history: the crossing loop at Forres was, from the 1960s to 2017, inconveniently located east of the passenger station, as seen in this view looking from the sole station platform on 5 April 2017. The line has now been shifted northwards to a new station with two platforms served by a much longer crossing loop, which can accommodate the longest freight trains in Britain (775 metres). *David Spaven*

Shortly beyond Orbliston, the railway again meets the main A96 trunk road at Lhanbryde, a Welsh-sounding name, believed to be Pictish in origin, meaning 'Church of St. Bride'. The train now heads due west towards Elgin.

Elgin: Cathedral City

Elgin is the administrative and commercial centre of Moray. It is an old town which played host to several Scottish kings including David I (who granted Royal Burgh status around 1130), William I, Alexander II and Alexander III. It is a former city because of its cathedral which was built on land granted by King Alexander II on the south side of the River Lossie. The foundation stone was laid in 1224 but, although its construction was completed sometime after 1242, it was destroyed by fire in 1270. The present-day ruins date from the subsequent rebuilding, the cathedral being abandoned in 1560 with services transferred to St Giles Church.

Today, the town's wide High Street includes the later 19th-century St Giles Church which was designed by Archibald Simpson. A short walk west from the High Street brings you to Dr.Gray's, the smallest District General Hospital in Scotland. It was built between 1815 and 1818 and includes a large classical block, with giant Doric columns supporting a portico, and topped with a drum tower and dome. The hospital had a £22 million refurbishment between 1992 and 1997.

As the train enters Elgin, you will see the B-listed former Great North station and the C-listed 'Elgin Centre' signal box on the right-hand side, both looking rather dilapidated and forlorn from the railway side. The signal box in particular is in poor condition, and there are moves afoot to persuade Network Rail and other stakeholders to pursue its restoration. Fortunately, the main station building has been

Traditional ironwork patterns at Forres station's single platform frame a freight train of barley wagons heading for Inverness on 9 May 1991. The newly realigned and straightened railway now runs eastwards (to the right) to the new station from around the point the locomotive is passing in this photo. *Bill Roberton*

renovated for office accommodation and has retained its imposing frontage and wonderful wood-panelled and stain glass internal former booking hall. The Highland Railway Company refused to share the cost of a joint station to replace the original antiquated structure opened in 1862, and so the Great North built this station on their own, opening in 1902.

The eastern end of the station served trains to Lossiemouth and the Moray Coast. Lossiemouth was the birthplace in 1866 of Ramsay MacDonald, the UK's first Labour Prime Minister, and the railway to Elgin was used by thousands of servicemen stationed at the local Royal Naval Air Station which is today's RAF Lossiemouth. The Elgin rail yards beyond the old Great North station were a hive of whisky-related activity until succumbing to road competition in 1992. However, following the successful operation of a trial train service to Grangemouth in 2013, called *Lifting the Spirit*, there are hopes that rail will once again take the pressure off the A9, A95, and A96 roads to the south.

Your train now enters the modern station (with its unusual avenue of trees on the platform) which was previously that of the Highland Railway. It was rebuilt in 1990 and looks over towards a modern retail park on the left. There is now no connection with the Victorian era. This station was linked to the Great North station for through running, and remains so today for access into the freight yard, which was used as a supply base for the line upgrading works between Elgin and Forres in 2017. It is a 10-minute walk from the station to Elgin town centre.

Elgin to Forres

Between Elgin and Forres the train passes through Mosstowie station (closed 1955), followed by Alves station which at one time handled significant amounts of agricultural freight. In the 1960s the Royal Train

The old Forres station seen from the eastern end of the platform on 9 May 1991. The 'starter' semaphore signal controlled the entry into the crossing loop east of the station. The platform's attractive canopy and adjacent 1955 station building are no longer in use, now that the railway has been re-routed to the north. *Bill Roberton*

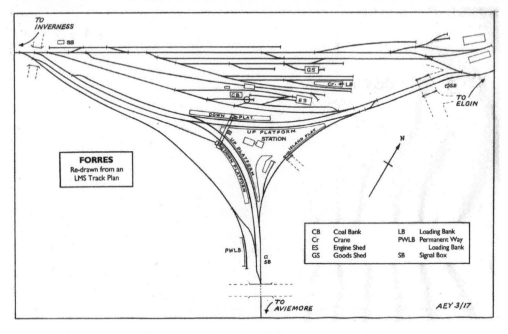

Alan Young's hand-drawn version of an LMSR (London, Midland & Scottish Railway) track plan shows the extensive layout at Forres which lasted until the mid-1960s, with a variety of passenger, freight and engineers' facilities in and around the station. *Alan Young*

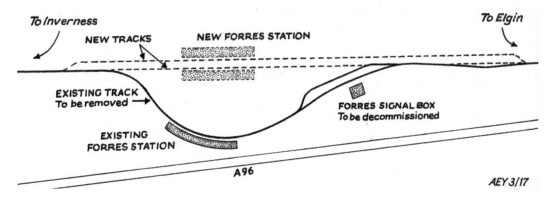

To Inverness

NEW TRACKS

NEW FORRES STATION

To Elgin

EXISTING TRACK
To be removed →

EXISTING
FORRES STATION

FORRES SIGNAL BOX
To be decommissioned

A96

AEY 3/17

A big contrast to the track layout in LMSR days, but the new route alignment and station relocation at Forres deliver a very significant improvement for passengers. The drastic reduction in infrastructure reflects changing technology (steam to diesel, local manual control to centralised electronic signalling), line closures (southwards over Dava Moor) and the concentration of rail freight and track maintenance facilities at the major centres of Aberdeen and Inverness. *Alan Young* occasionally called to deliver or collect Prince Charles to nearby Gordonstoun school. A branch north from Alves to Burghead opened in 1862 and was extended to Hopeman in 1892 but it closed to passengers in 1931. Diageo's Burghead maltings date back to 1966 and it – and the more modern Roseisle maltings – used the line for conveyance of barley until 1992, but thereafter it fell into disuse.

The new Roseisle Distillery, barely visible in the distant countryside to your right, was the largest distillery to be built for over 30 years. It opened in 2010 with a capacity of ten million litres per annum, producing spirit for Diageo's Johnnie Walker and Buchanan blends.

On the far horizon over the Moray Firth you can see the mountains of Sutherland and, further to the north, Caithness. Morven, the highest point of Caithness, is particularly distinctive. Another short branch (three miles) was constructed from the next station, Kinloss, to Findhorn but it was short-lived from 1861 to 1869. Very little of the line remains, as much was covered when Kinloss Airfield was built in 1938-39. RAF Kinloss ceased flying operations in 2011, but the runways are maintained for relief purposes and the Army have used the accommodation in recent years. You can see the village and bay of Findhorn in the distance. The village is well known for the Findhorn Foundation, a Scottish charitable trust formed in 1972 by the spiritual community at the Ecovillage.

On the right of the former Kinloss station (closed 1965) you can see the ruins of Kinloss Abbey, founded by King David 1 in 1150 and initially colonised by the monks of Melrose Abbey in the Scottish Borders. Three miles east of Forres, it became one of the largest Cistercian monasteries in Scotland, and its great wealth was in part due to the grant of salmon fishing rights on the River Findhorn by Robert the Bruce in 1312.

As the train nears Forres you will see the 70-foot octagonal Cluny Tower on the hill above the town to the left. It was built in 1806 by public subscription as a tribute to Admiral Lord Nelson. It is currently open

The graceful style of Nairn station seen from the entrance to 'The Coffee Station' café on 5 April 2017. *David Spaven*

to the public between 14.00 and 16.00 every day from April to September. Those who make the effort to climb to the top are rewarded with stunning 360-degree views, particularly to Caithness in the north and towards Ullapool in the west (*See Chapter Five for contact details*).

Forres: Royal Burgh

As the train enters the new Forres crossing loop, you will see Mosset Park on the left side. This is the home of Forres Mechanics FC, the oldest surviving football club in the North of Scotland, having been formed in 1884. In 1893 they were founder members of the Scottish Highland Football League in which they still compete. There has been much speculation over the years as to the origin of the club name. It was too early to be connected with the car industry and, although some believe there was a link to local railway workers, in the 19th century 'mechanic' was a wider term used in association with both general machinery workers and tradesmen.

Benromach Distillery appears to your right. It was built in 1898 by Charles Doig (note his trademark pagoda) and, although closed between 1983 and 1998, it is in full production today. Following the opening of the new crossing loop and station, the train now bypasses the old station, which originally was the three-sided junction for the Highland Railway's main line south to Perth via Dava Moor and Grantown-on-Spey. That line opened in 1863 and closed in 1965 as part of the Beeching cuts. There was direct access from both the east and west ends of the Aberdeen – Inverness railway. In the days of steam, Forres housed the 'banking' locomotives which assisted the Highland Railway's main line trains to ascend the infamous and wild Dava Moor to the summit 17 miles to the south.

The footbridge at Nairn offers an attractive view towards the main station building and its distinctive chimney stacks, seen on 5 April 2017, with 'The Coffee Station' café housed at the far end of the building. *David Spaven*

Forres is one of Scotland's oldest towns, having been awarded Royal Burgh status in 1140. On 23 June 1496, James IV of Scotland granted a Royal Charter which set out the rights and privileges to be enjoyed by the inhabitants. Forres was once a major market town as evidenced by its wide main street, and its former wealth is reflected in its many fine buildings.

Forres to Nairn

The train crosses the River Findhorn shortly after departure from Forres. The B-listed triple-span box girder-style bridge was designed by Joseph Mitchell but its steel enclosure precludes any real view of the river or countryside.

To the right (north) of the railway lies the vast Culbin Forest, covering 9,000 acres between Findhorn Bay and Nairn. Originally the largest dune system in Britain and marginal farmland, this area was abandoned after being buried in sand following a huge storm in 1694. The Forestry Commission took possession in the 1920s and, by planting Scots and Corsican pine and Norwegian spruce, have gradually transformed the land into today's remarkable landscape. The forest is a haven for wildlife, including roe deer, breeding crested tits, red squirrels, and the elusive pine marten, and can be visited all year round for walking and cycling. Some trails are marked and, if you crave peace, quiet, and tranquillity, Culbin Forest is worth a visit. It is designated a Site of Special Scientific Interest (SSSI). The beach wasn't so peaceful during World War Two as it was used for D-Day training.

The train rattles past the former station of Brodie (closed 1965) and the back of the popular Brodie Countryfare visitor centre which incorporates a large restaurant. Brodie Castle, a National Trust for

The B-listed Nairn West signal box seen looking west towards Inverness on 16 September 1977, when it was still operational and goods traffic was being handled in the sidings beyond. *Bill Roberton*

Scotland property, is nearby. It dates from the 16th century and was the home of the Clan Brodie. It is full of antique furniture, paintings and ceramics within a 71-hectare estate.

The climate in this area is relatively mild, and often local farmers are combining in the summer months at the same time as their counterparts in the south of England. The downside, however, is that the dry conditions regularly result in soil erosion and dust storms. A few miles west of Brodie the train leaves Moray. Welcome to the Highlands. The train speeds through Auldearn (closed 1960) and Nairn awaits.

Nairn: Seaside County Town

Nairn, at one time the County Town of Nairnshire, is a former herring port and market town. In the 19th century the Victorians flocked here, attracted by the supposed medicinal benefits of the sea waters. Today, Nairn is known for its fine beaches and golf courses.

The train crosses high above the River Nairn on a B-listed four-arch viaduct as it slows. Nairn station was renowned for its two signal boxes, East and West (also protected by their B-listed status), at either ends of the lengthy northern platform. Passengers were afforded the sight of railway staff cycling between the two boxes to operate the points and signals to allow trains to proceed. That practice continued until the early years of the current century.

The elegant Victorian station buildings, also B-listed, date back to 1855 and reflect Nairn's growing 19th-century status as a seaside resort of note. In 1970 the station masqueraded as Inverness in Billy Wilder's film 'The Private Life of Sherlock Holmes' starring Robert Stephens, Christopher Lee and Colin Blakely. The building on the southern platform, formerly a flower shop, is now used by Nairn Men's Shed

Nairn station was famous for its two signal boxes, East and West, at either end of the lengthy main (northern) platform. These controlled the points and signals throughout the station area and for decades passengers were afforded the sight of the signalman cycling between the two boxes to activate the equipment to allow trains to proceed. This practice – seen on 17 July 1992 – continued until the early years of the 21st century! Both boxes are B-Listed and have recently been refurbished. *Bill Roberton*

group, a concept which originated in Australia to bring men together to exercise practical skills and to combat social isolation. (The Nairn group make it clear that they also welcome women!)

Immediately to the south of the station (on your left) is the home of another Highland League Football Club, Nairn County FC. Appropriately, the ground is named 'Station Park'. The present day club was founded in 1914 and the timing was unfortunate. The club was granted admittance to the Highland League on 31 July 1914 and on 4 August their first competitive fixture at home to Citadel of Inverness was announced. But literally within hours that same day Britain declared war on Germany, and both Nairn County and the Highland League were forced to abandon football for the duration. Nairn County had the rather dubious distinction of taking a full five years to play their first league match – which they lost 4-0 at home to Inverness Thistle on 13 September 1919. The attendance was over 600, with many of the 'visitors' arriving conveniently by train at the adjacent station. They were by no means the last to do so.

Nairn to Inverness

The journey now enters its final 16 miles to Inverness over relatively open and level countryside. Cawdor Castle lies three miles south of the line and was provided with its own station named Kildrummie, but it closed as early as 1858. The castle is associated with Shakespeare's 'Scottish play' *Macbeth*, as the title character was appointed 'Thane of Cawdor', but the association is fictionalised and there is no direct reference to Cawdor Castle in the play.

The line passes underneath the A96 trunk road fly-over at Gollanfield (closed 1965). Originally, this station was named Fort George until the short branch to the garrison was opened in 1899, at which

Hauled by a Class 47 locomotive, on 17 July 1992 a trainload of barley wagons bursts into the open past the original Highland Railway goods shed at Nairn. *Bill Roberton*

point it was renamed Gollanfield Junction. The branch line ran for over one mile and actually terminated in Ardersier, approximately the same distance from the Fort. Public passenger services were withdrawn in 1943 but troop trains continued until complete closure in 1958. Unfortunately, Gollanfield is also remembered for a fatal collision in 1953 between an eastbound passenger and westbound goods, in which three railwaymen were killed.

To the north you are now afforded a wonderful view across the Moray Firth to the Black Isle. This is a misnomer, for the 'Isle' is actually a peninsula which reputedly takes its name from its dark appearance even during periods of snow. Beyond the Black Isle and clearly visible from the train (in good weather) are the steep slopes of Ben Wyvis (3,432 feet). These stand out impressively in winter snow and provide Invernessians with a weather barometer: 'snow on the Ben' is a local phrase, indicating that winter is arriving in the Inverness area. The Black Isle and Ben Wyvis remain in view over the last few remaining miles into Inverness.

To the left of the railway lies the planned 'new town' of Tornagrain. Conceived over 10 years ago in response to the rapid growth of the Inverness area, a community of 12,000, incorporating all main services, is projected and the first residents moved into their homes in 2017. A short distance further on the line passes Inverness (Dalcross) Airport on your right. The airfield was constructed in 1940 as RAF Dalcross and opened for civilian flights in 1947. Dalcross station closed in 1965 but there are current plans to build a new station to serve the airport, industrial estate, and major new housing developments.

A couple of miles further on, to the right, you can see Castle Stuart, a Scottish tower house completed by the 3rd Earl of Moray in 1625. It was built on land granted to the 1st Earl by his half-sister Mary Queen of Scots in 1561, but his murder and that of his son-in-law, the 2nd Earl, delayed progress somewhat. As the fortunes of the House of Stuart waned in the 17th and 18th century, the house fell into disuse and lay

The fine B-listed station buildings, footbridge and signal box at Nairn, looking west towards Inverness. *Merrill MacWilliam (from a photo by David Fasken)*

derelict for over 300 years. In modern times it has been renovated and used as both a private residence and luxury hotel.

On your left is one of the largest manufacturing sites in the Highlands: the Dalcross plant of Norbord, where timber from across the region is converted into panel products. A £95m expansion is underway, and it is hoped that a direct rail connection will be provided, helping to reduce the number of heavy lorries on the roads. The train then passes the former station at Allanfearn (closed 1965) and approaches its destination.

Inverness: Highland Capital

As the train approaches the outskirts of the city, you may spot to the right (below the Kessock Bridge) the relatively new stadium of Inverness Caledonian Thistle FC who play in the Scottish League. The club was formed in 1994 following the amalgamation of two of the town's three Highland League clubs Caledonian and Thistle (the third, Clachnacuddin FC, remain in the Scottish Highland Football League). At the time it was not an easy marriage, as over a century of rivalry, history, tradition and mistrust had to be overcome before the new club was born.

Part of the football ground is built on the former site of Longman Airport which was built in 1933 as a civilian airfield for Highland Airways. Originally intended, but seldom used, for flying boats using the adjacent waters of the Moray Firth, the airport saw the commencement of the first regular services north to Wick and Orkney that year. The return flights into Inverness allowed passengers to connect with southbound trains. In 1941 the airfield was designated RAF Longman (or RAF Inverness) and was strategically positioned to defend the Caledonian Canal and north of Scotland fuel supplies. It also served

In April 2017 the wooden station building on the southern platform at Nairn (formerly a waiting room) was transitioning to a 'Men's Shed' – the first on a British railway station – offering men of all ages a place where they can talk and pursue new hobbies. The facility at Nairn will include a workshop for metalwork and woodwork and a room to develop IT skills. *Merrill MacWilliam (from a photo by David Spaven)*

as a 'relief' airfield for Kinloss and Lossiemouth. It was returned to the civil aviation authorities in 1946 but was considered too small for safe operations and was closed in 1947. All operations were transferred to today's airport at Dalcross. Very little survives from those pioneering days of flying, as the entire area has been developed as a modern industrial and retail complex in recent years.

To the north of the football stadium, the A9 Kessock Bridge dominates the skyline and is clearly visible from the train. It was built in 1982 to replace the small car ferry which plied the narrow stretch of firth between South and North Kessock. Invernessians today still harbour memories of the 'Rosehaugh' and 'Eilean Dubh' vessels.

The train runs under the Highland Main Line south to Aviemore and Perth and the A9 trunk road, before passing Millburn and Welsh's Bridge Junctions where the lines from the east and south merge. To the right, you may spot the snowploughs which are attached to diesel locomotives in winter to keep the Highland railways open. You will also see the new railhead, which handles Tesco supermarket supplies which have arrived by rail from the south, with the distinctive 'Stobart' and 'Less CO_2' brandings.

The train enters Inverness station alongside Lochgorm Works (to your right) which date back to the original Inverness and Nairn Railway in 1855, and which are still used today for train maintenance. Inverness station has also retained its historical triangular lay-out with its platforms fanning out from the main station concourse. Platforms 1-4 serve the Perth and Aberdeen lines and Platforms 5-7 the line to Dingwall and thence north to Wick and Thurso and west to Kyle of Lochalsh. The triangle is completed by the 'Rose Street Curve' on the third side. This affords flexibility by allowing trains from both south/east and north/west to bypass the station and reverse into the platforms at the opposite ends. This practice was used in the past for through running rolling stock and, in the days of locomotive hauled trains (both steam and diesel), to prevent the engine from being 'trapped' at the concourse end of the platform.

A snow-clad Class 20 locomotive stands at the western end of Millburn Yard, Inverness in the winter of 1974-75. The hill in the background – in the town's Crown district – is reputed to have been the location of King Macbeth's castle. *David Spaven*

After alighting from the train, and as you approach the ticket barrier, you will notice two interesting plaques on either side of the wall dividing Platforms 4 and 5: one depicts the Inverness & Aberdeen Junction Railway Company crest and directors, and the other commemorates the final Highland Railway link between Nairn and Keith in 1858.

You have arrived in the Highland Capital with the opportunity to explore the town which was re-designated a city 17 years ago. The station is in Academy Street in the heart of the 'Old Town' with easy access to the castle, river area, cathedral, Victorian market, shops and restaurants. The imposing and architecturally splendid Town House, recently renovated, was built in Flemish-Baronial style from 1878 to 1882 and, although not now used by the Council, it hosts meetings, civil functions and marriages, and concerts.

Its main claim to fame was that, until 2008, it was the only building in the United Kingdom outside of London to host a Cabinet Meeting. Prime Minister David Lloyd George was on holiday in Gairloch in September 1921 when Southern Ireland threatened to secede from the United Kingdom. Rather than return to London, he convened a cabinet meeting in the Town House, and the resulting 'Inverness Formula' provided the basis for the establishment of the Irish Free State.

Eden Court Theatre on the banks of the River Ness (opened 1976) offers a range of theatre, cinema and arts. The main Tourist Information Centre is in Castle Wynd (beside the Town House) and supplies a full range of detail on the city and the wider Highlands as well as accommodation. You can even book a cruise on Loch Ness for some monster spotting.

Alternatively, you can change for rail services to the south, to Kyle of Lochalsh on the west coast (as featured in a companion *Insider Rail Guide* to this volume), or to Caithness (the Far North Line, whose history is told in *Highland Survivor* by David Spaven, another publication from Kessock Books).

DIRECTORS

ALEX. MATHESON, ESQ. OF ARDROSS, M.P. CHAIRMAN.
THE RIGHT HON. THE EARL OF SEAFIELD.
GEO. LOCH, ESQ. LONDON.
ENEAS W. MACKINTOSH, ESQ. OF RAIGMORE.
SIR JAMES. D. H. ELPHINSTONE, BART. M. P.
WM. JAS. TAYLOR, ESQ. OF ROTHIEMAY.
SIR ALEX. P. GORDON CUMMING, BART. OF ALTYRE.

DIRECTORS

THE HON. THOS. CHAS. BRUCE. DEPUTY-CHAIRMAN.
ALEX. INGLIS. ROBERTSON. ESQ. OF AULTNASKIACH.
THE RIGHT HON. THE EARL OF CAITHNESS.
CAPTAIN WM. FRASER-TYTLER OF ALDOURIE.
THE MOST NOBLE THE MARQUIS OF STAFFORD. M.P.
JOHN BLAIKIE, ESQ. ABERDEEN.
THE HON. GEORGE SKENE DUFF OF MILTONDUFF.

The 1858 plaque, adjacent to Platform 4 at Inverness station, listing the Directors of the Inverness & Aberdeen Junction Railway. *David Spaven*

The plaque, adjacent to Platform 5 at Inverness station, commemorating the 1858 opening of the Inverness & Aberdeen Junction Railway. *David Spaven*

CHAPTER FIVE

Selected features / Further reading

Aberdeen – A-listed station and overbridge; B-listed railway building on the corner of Guild Street and College Street (today a hairdresser), which was built in 1909 as a suburban ticket office providing direct access by stairs to Platform 9, to relieve congestion in the main concourse and booking hall area of the 'Joint Station'; War Memorial to Great North of Scotland Railway (GNSR) employees in the connecting passage between the station concourse and Union Square shopping mall.

Dyce – Aberdeen International Airport and heliport. Tall signal box.

Inverurie – B-listed station buildings and B-listed former Locomotive Works.

Insch – B-listed station building and overbridge; Insch Connection Museum (www.inschmuseum.org.uk)

Huntly – 10-minute walk to Huntly Castle (www.historicenvironment.scot/visit-a-place/places/huntly-castle)

Keith – 10-minute walk to Keith Town Station for Keith & Dufftown Railway (heritage line)   (www.keith-dufftown-railway.co.uk); 10-minute walk to Strathisla Distillery Visitor Centre (www.visitscotland.com/info/see-do/strathisla-distillery)

Elgin – B-listed former GNSR station at Elgin East; 10-minute walk to Elgin Cathedral (ruined)

Forres – new station opened October 2017; Cluny Tower (www.forresheritage.org.uk)

Nairn – B-listed station buildings (both platforms); two signal boxes and overbridge

Inverness – Inverness & Aberdeen Junction Railway 1858 commemoration plaque; original Highland Railway Lochgorm Works building in the track "triangle" beyond the station

Further Reading

As well as our own knowledge of the railway, gathered over more than 50 years – and my research for *If Goalposts Could Talk … The Life & Times of Inverurie Locomotive Works Football Club* – this guide has benefited enormously from the detailed research and writing of a variety of authors, notably:

- Alfred H. Forbes, *Time Does Transfix: Recollections of a Forres Railwayman* (1997)
- Great North of Scotland Railway Association, *Great North Memories Vols. 1 & 2* (1978 & 1981)
- ARB Haldane, *The Drove Roads of Scotland* (1973)
- Graeme MacLeod, Donald Wilson and Bill Logan, *The History of Nairn County F.C.* (2014)
- Bill McAllister, *Highland Hundred* (1993)
- Ian McKenzie and Alistair Coull, *The Whisky Line: A Guide to the Keith & Dufftown Railway* (2009)
- Michael Pearson, *Iron Road to Whisky Country* (2002)
- Ron Smith (Keith & District Heritage Group), *The Hush Hush* (2011)
- John Thomas and David Turnock, *A Regional History of the Railways of Great Britain, Volume 15* (1989)
- HA Vallance, *The Great North of Scotland Railway* (1965)
- Colin G. Watson, *Forres Mechanics: The First Hundred Years (1984)*

A modern plaque, adjacent to Platform 5 at Inverness station, celebrates two of the Highland Railway's greatest civil engineers. *David Spaven*